How to Draw for Kids

Young Scholar

Young Scholar
An imprint of Ciparum LLC

How to Draw for Kids
© 2017 Ciparum LLC
All rights reserved.
ISBN-10: 1-63589-489-1
ISBN-13: 978-1-63589-489-9

www.youngscholar.co

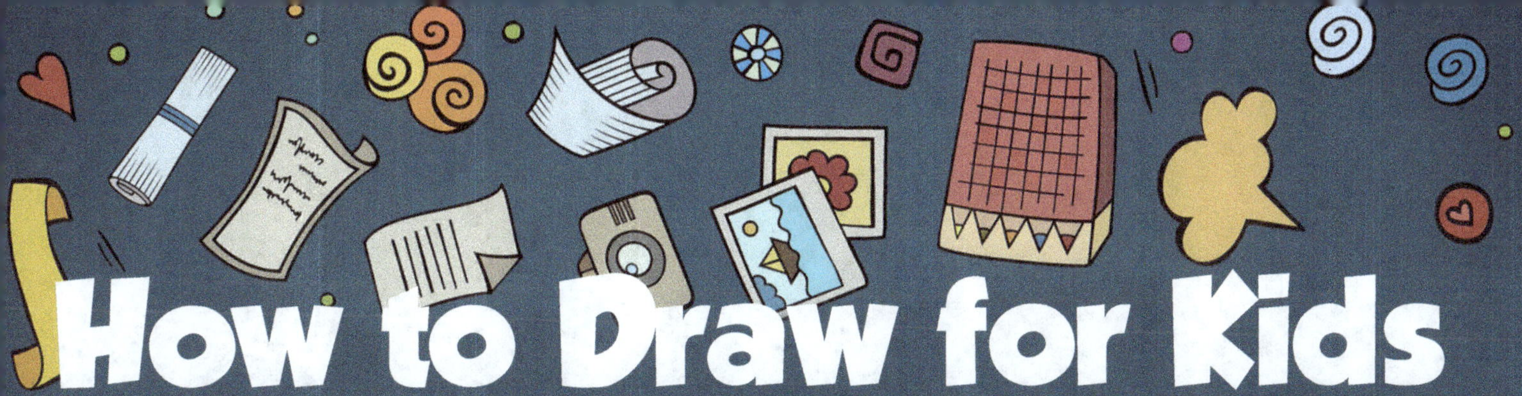

Table of Contents

Alligator

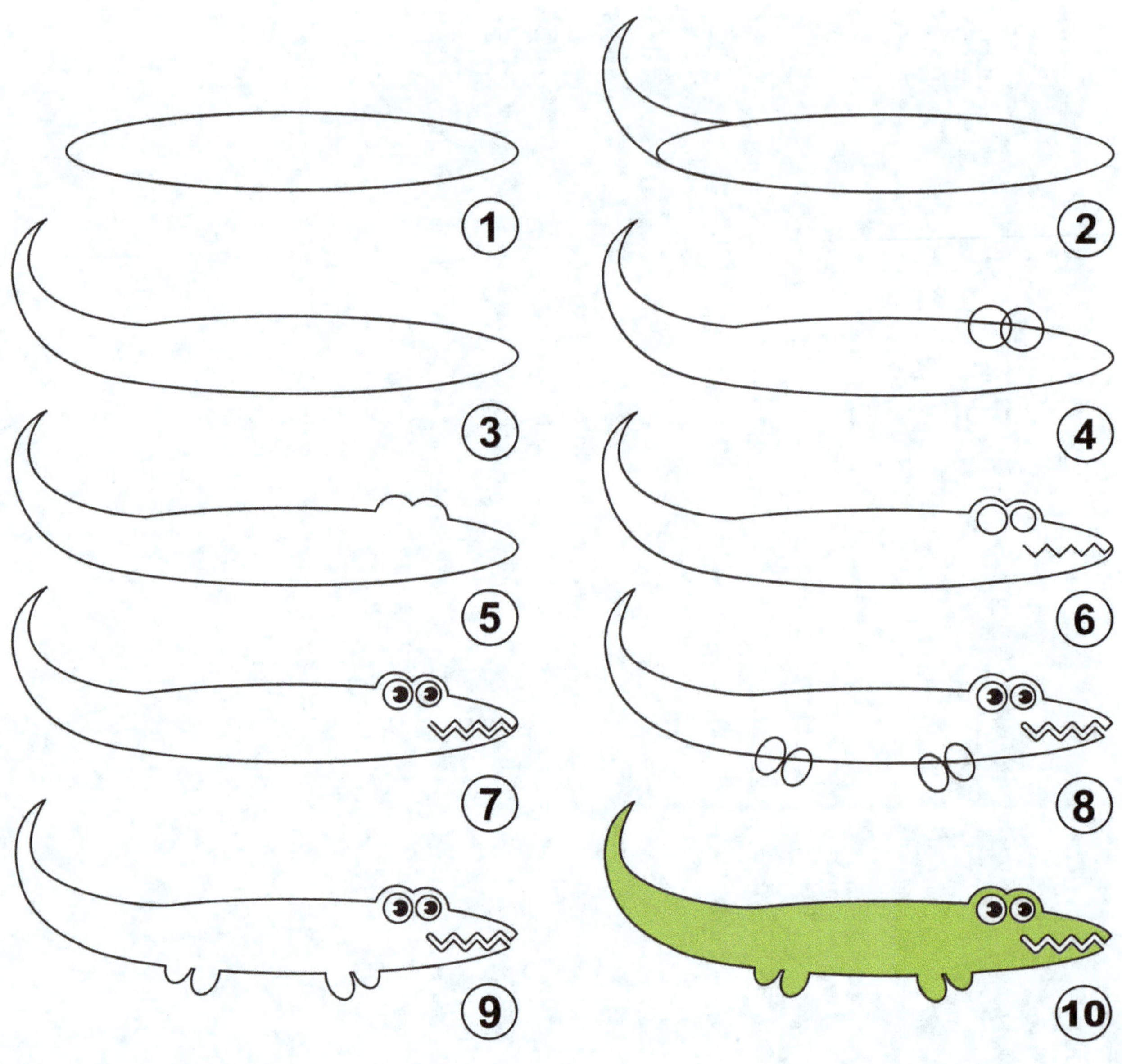

Ant

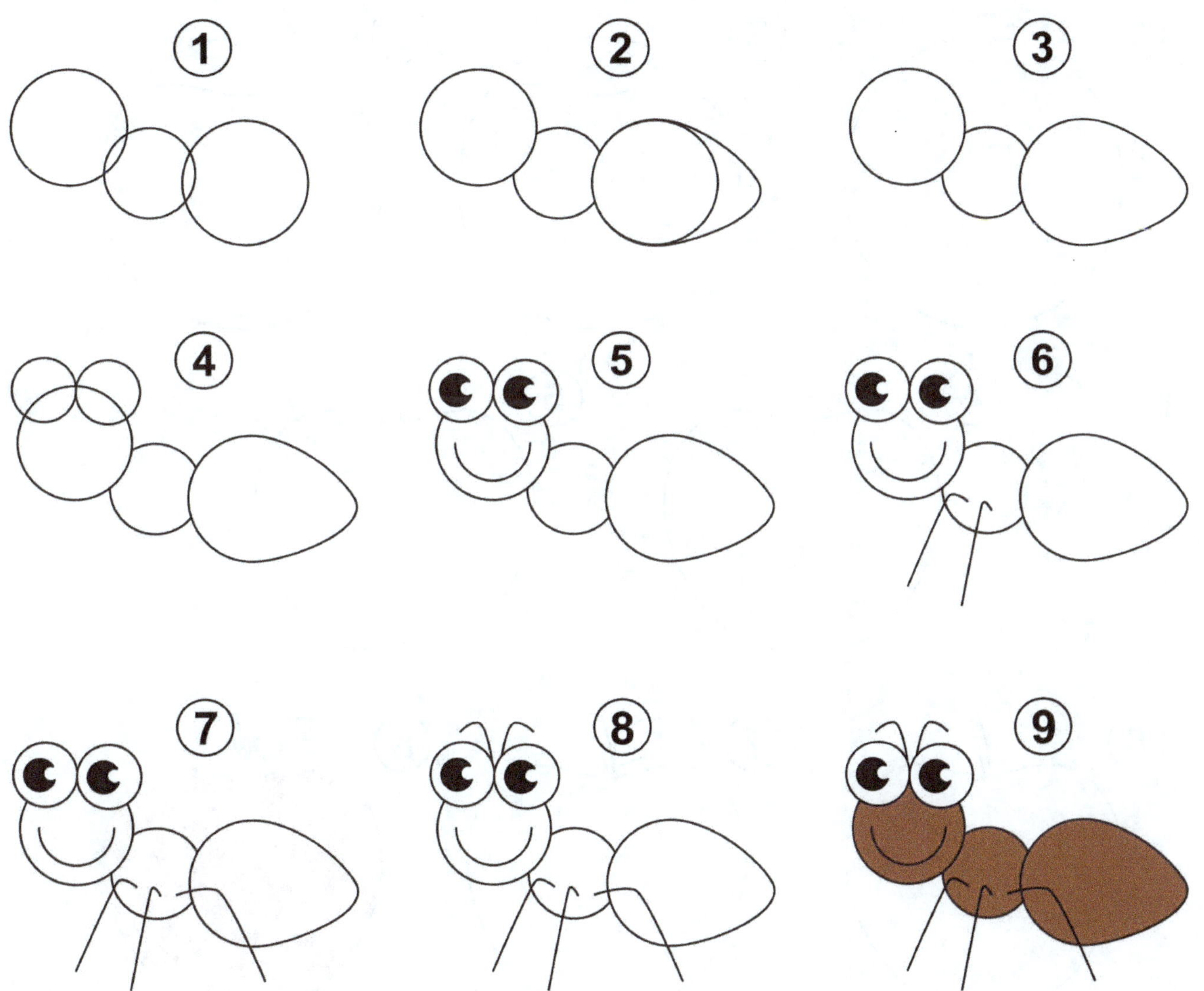

Apple

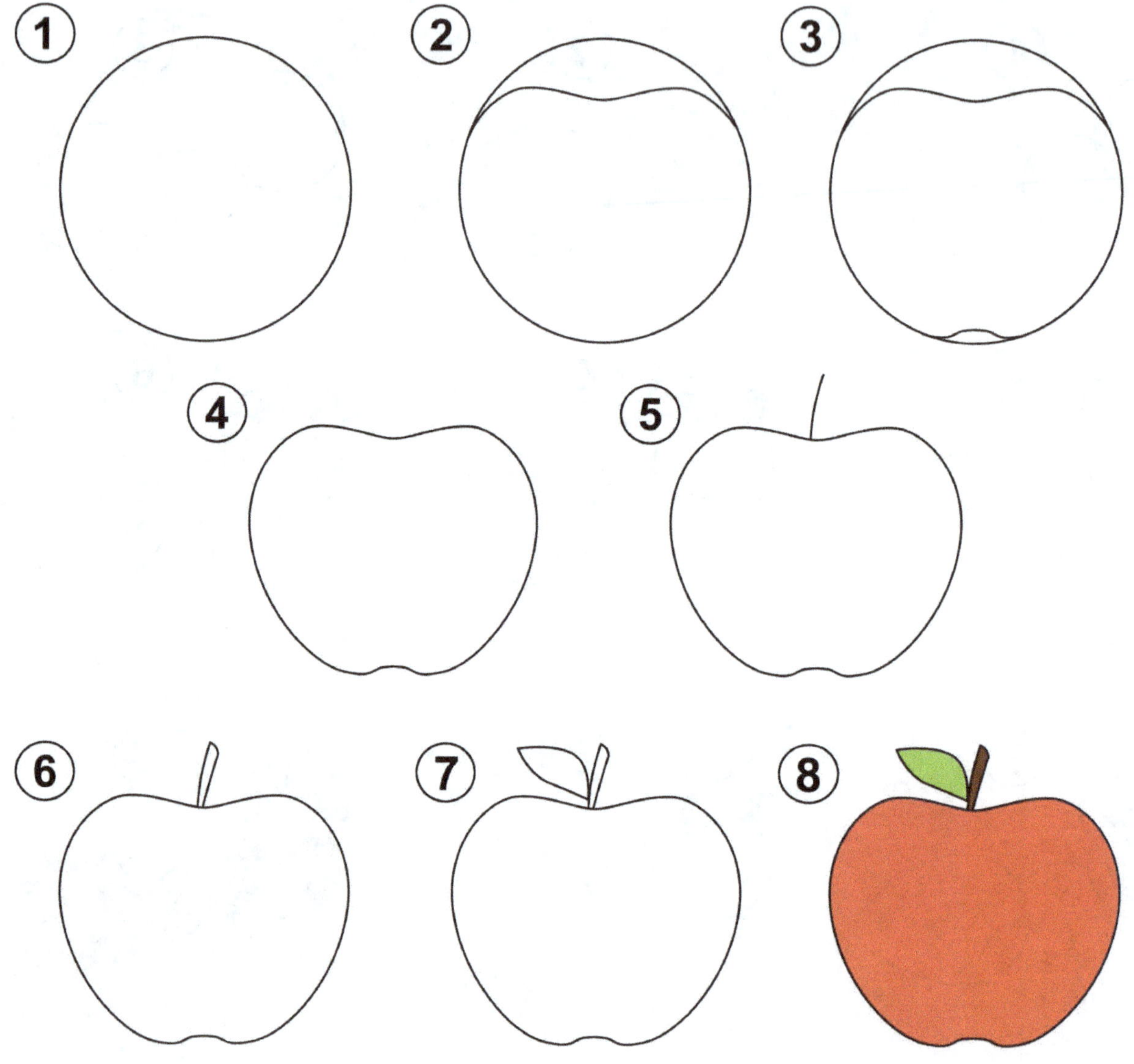

Balloons

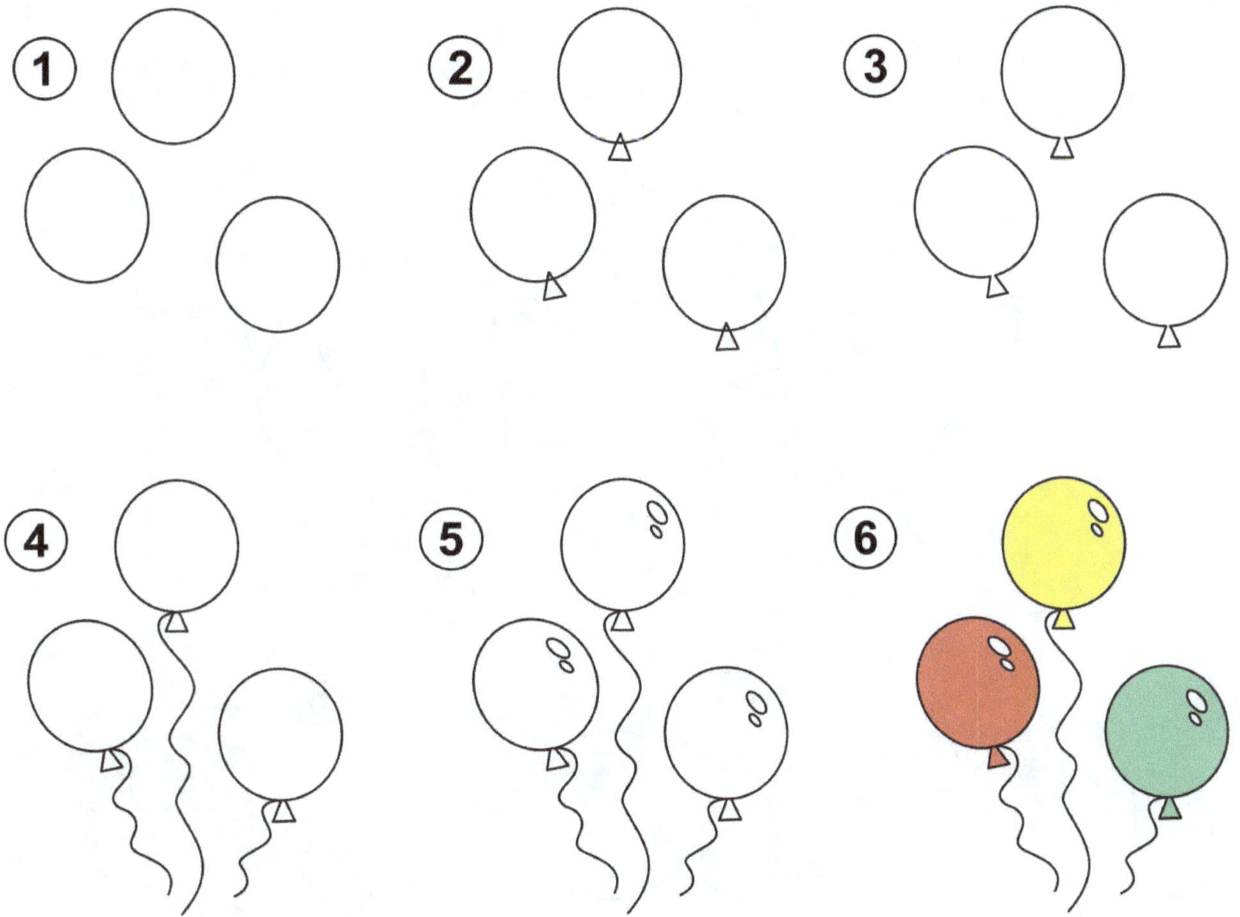

Bird

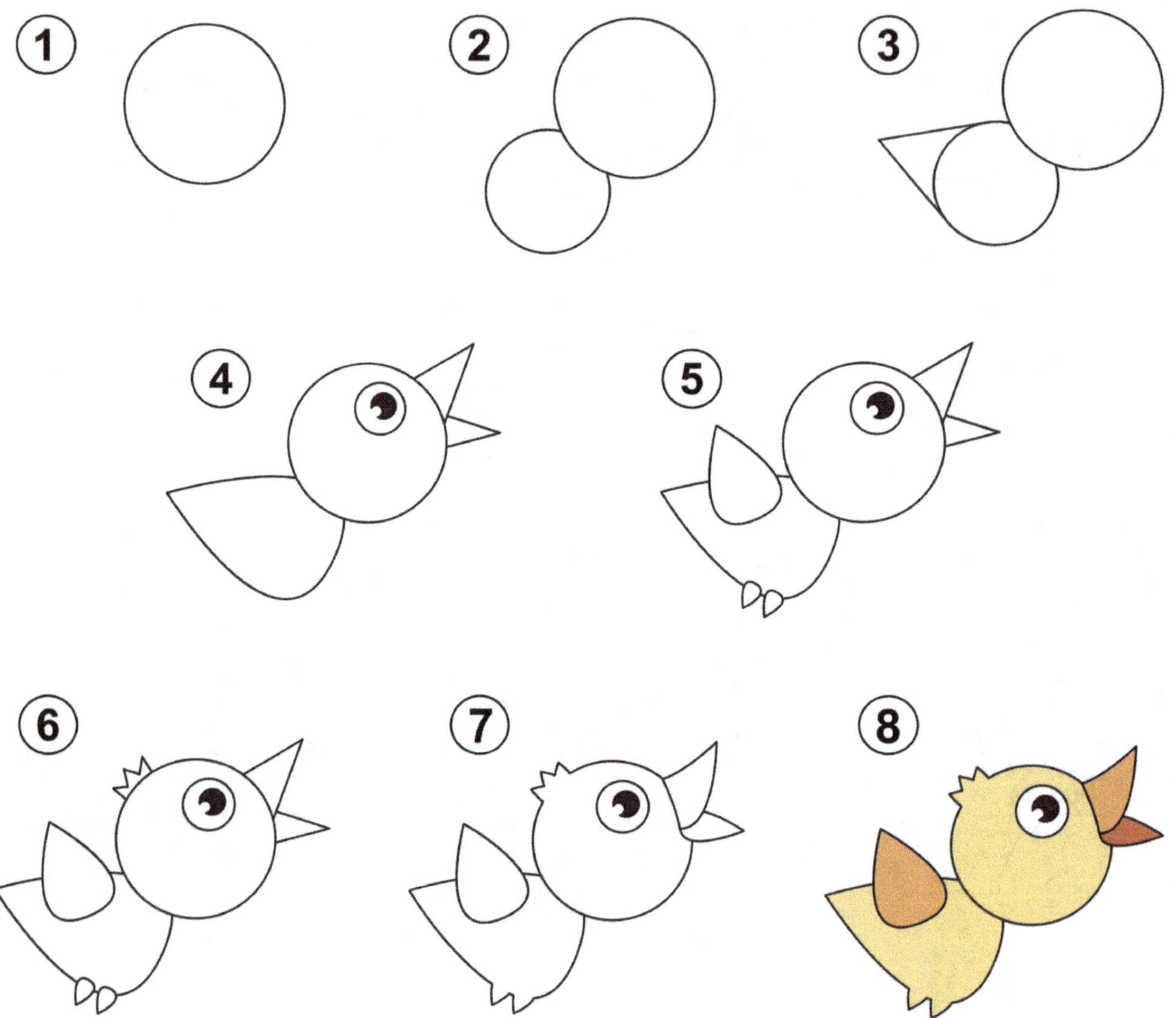

Blossom Branch

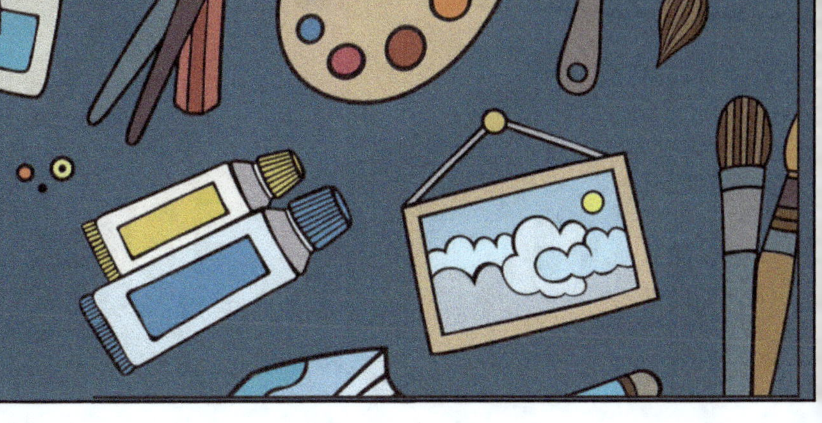

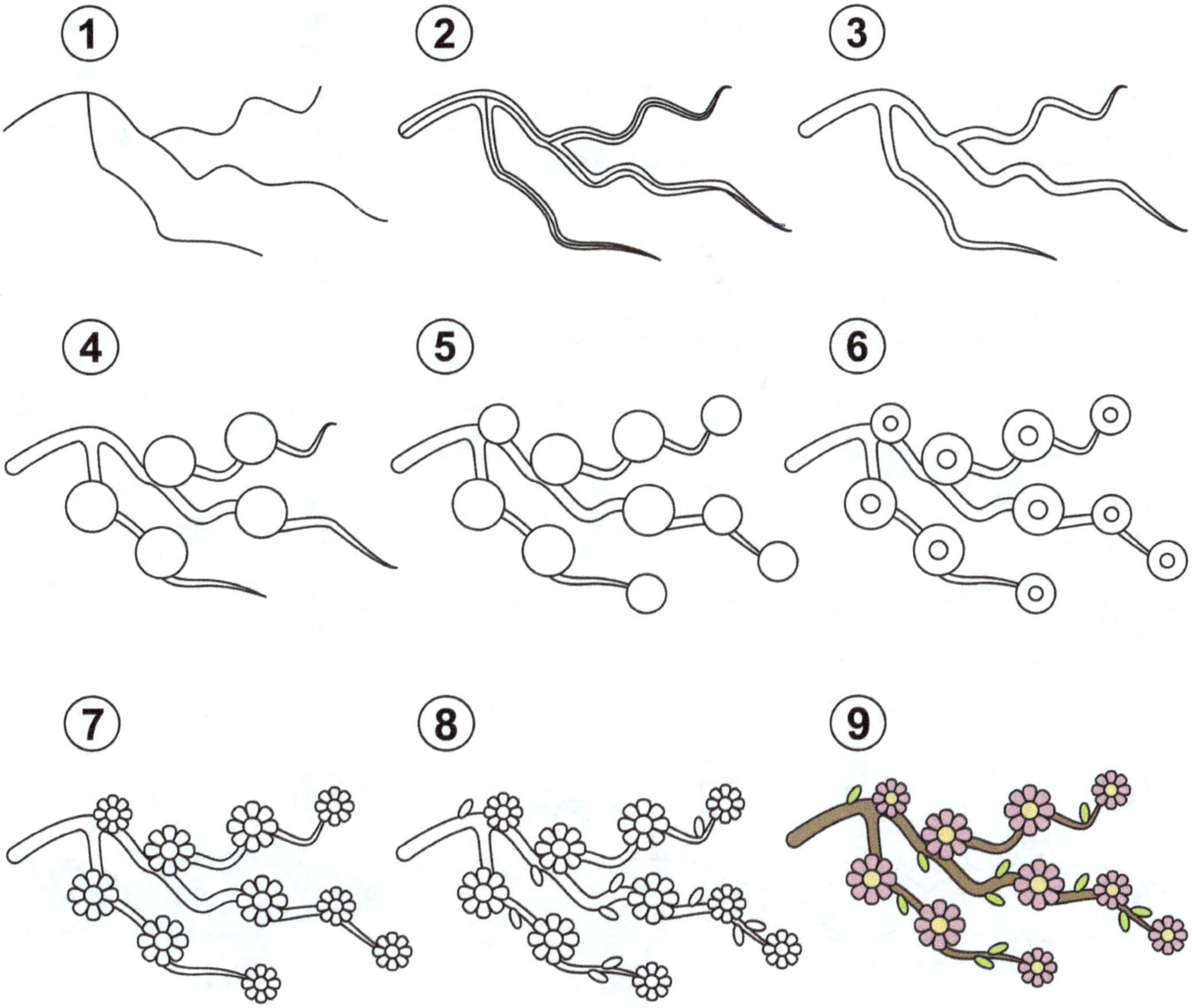

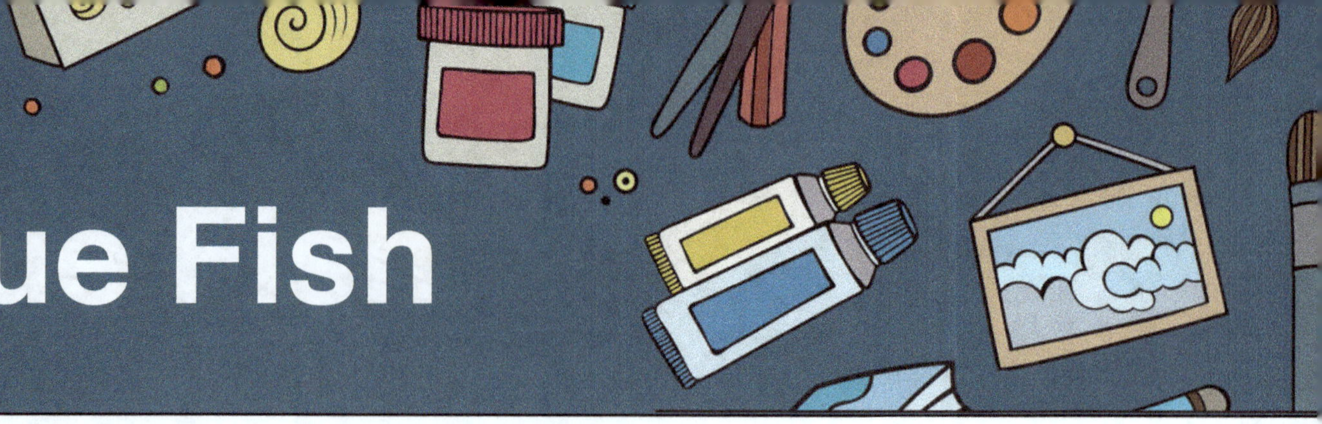

Blue Fish

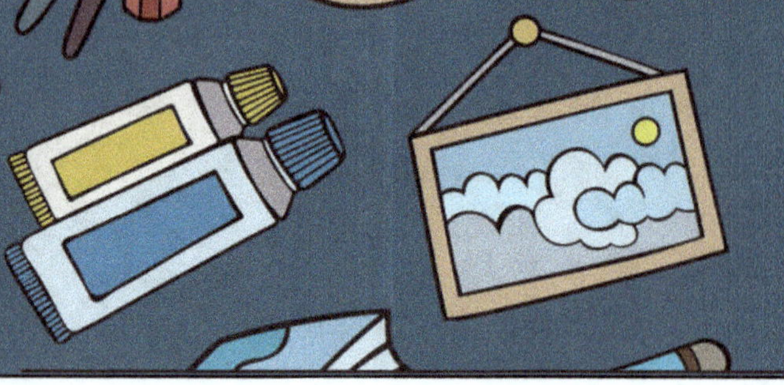

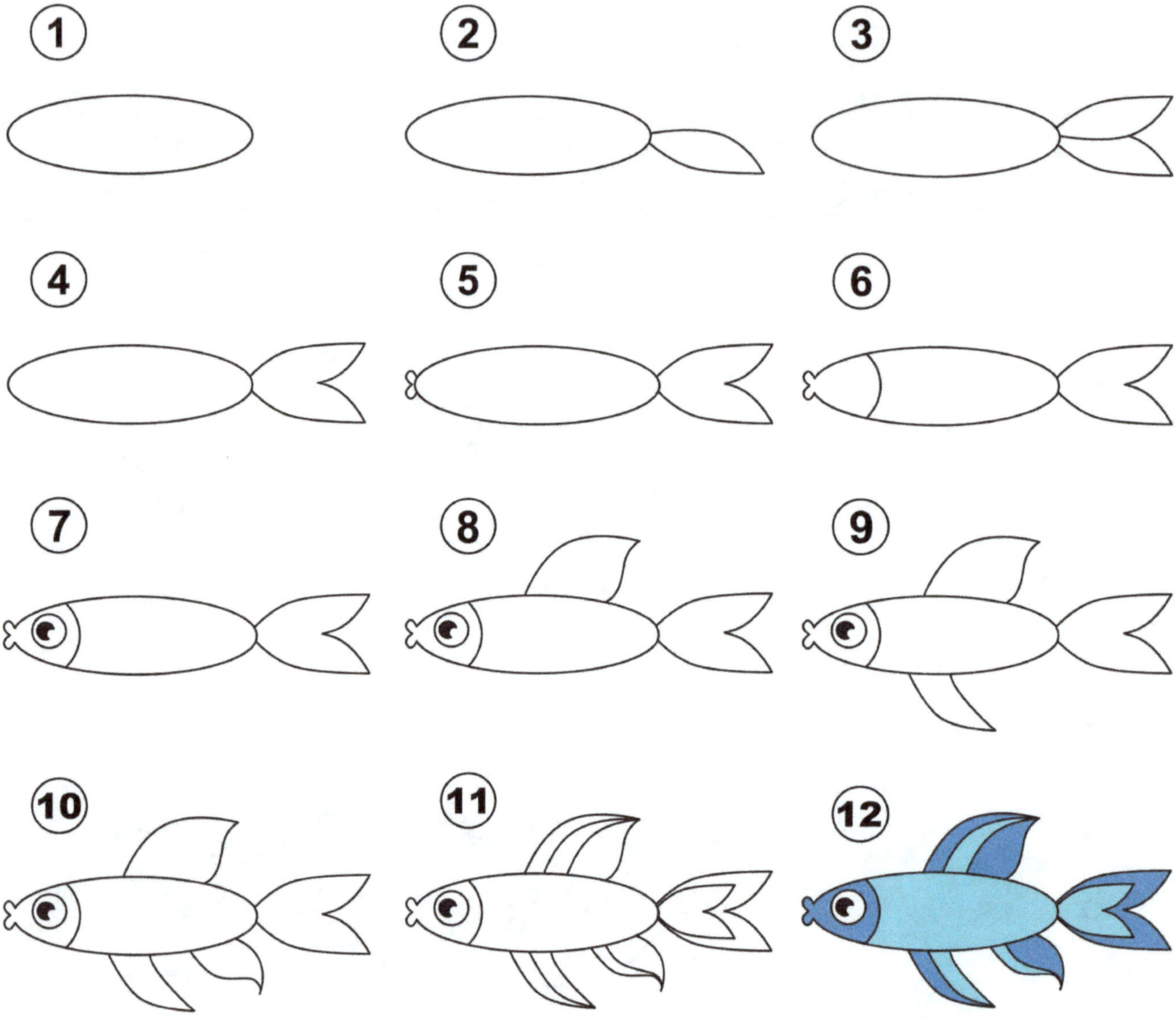

1

2

3

4

5

6

7

8

9

10

11

12

Bluebell Flower

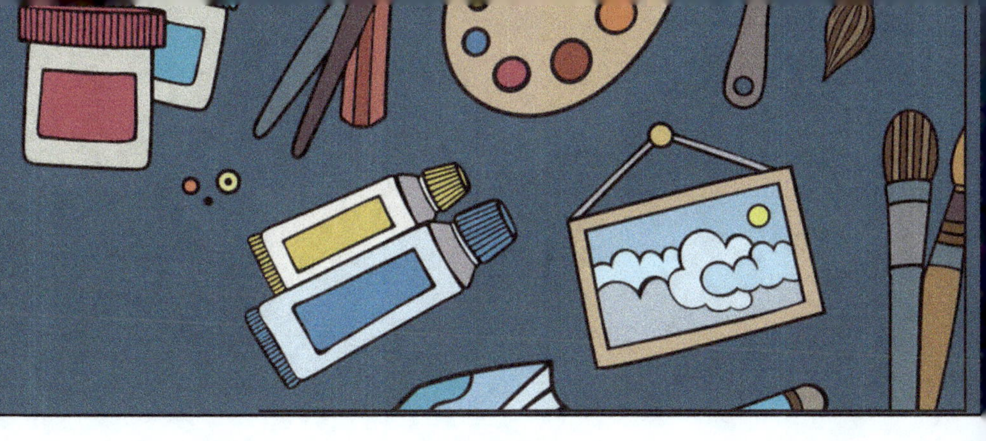

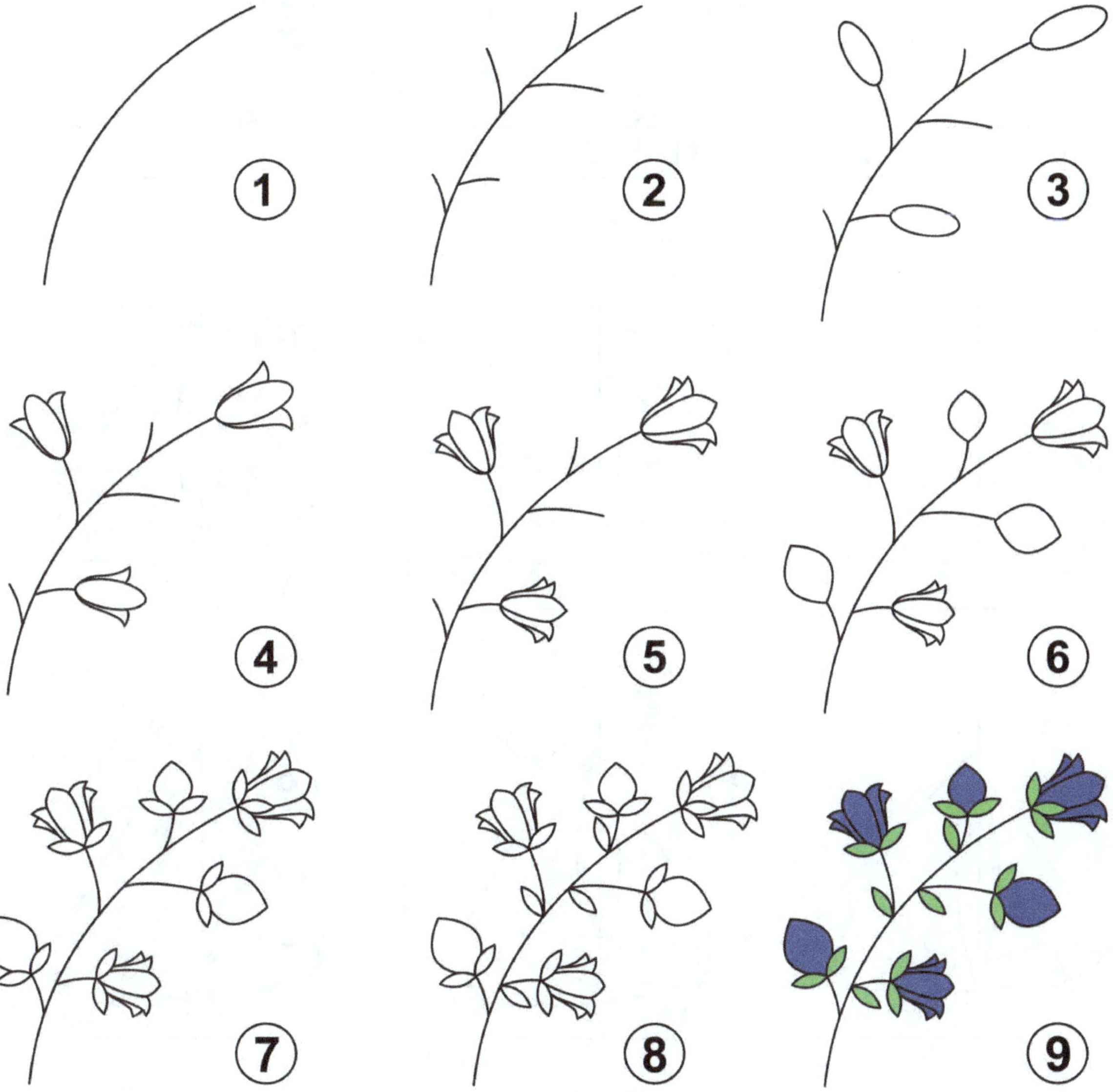

Boat

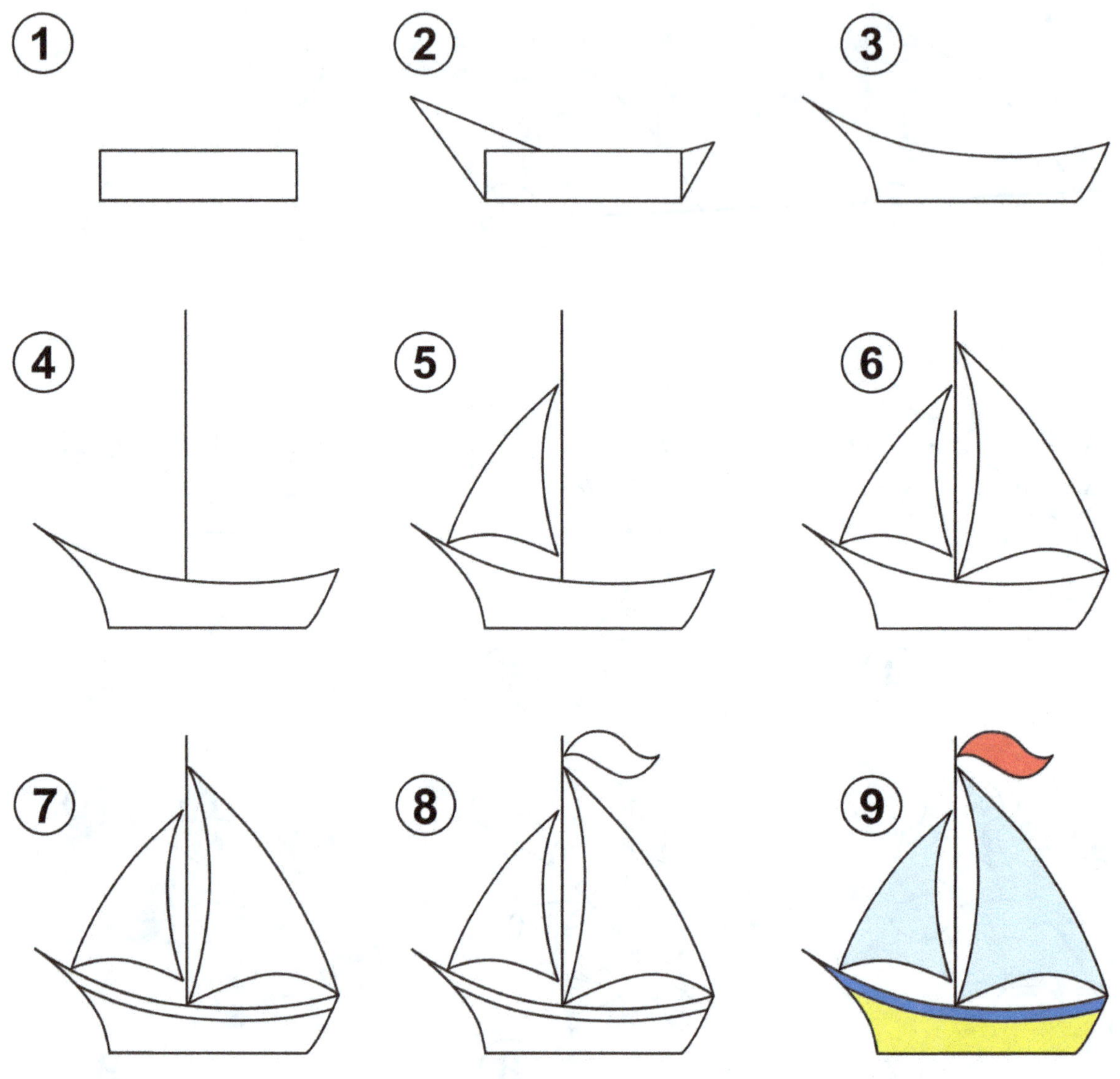

Bottle

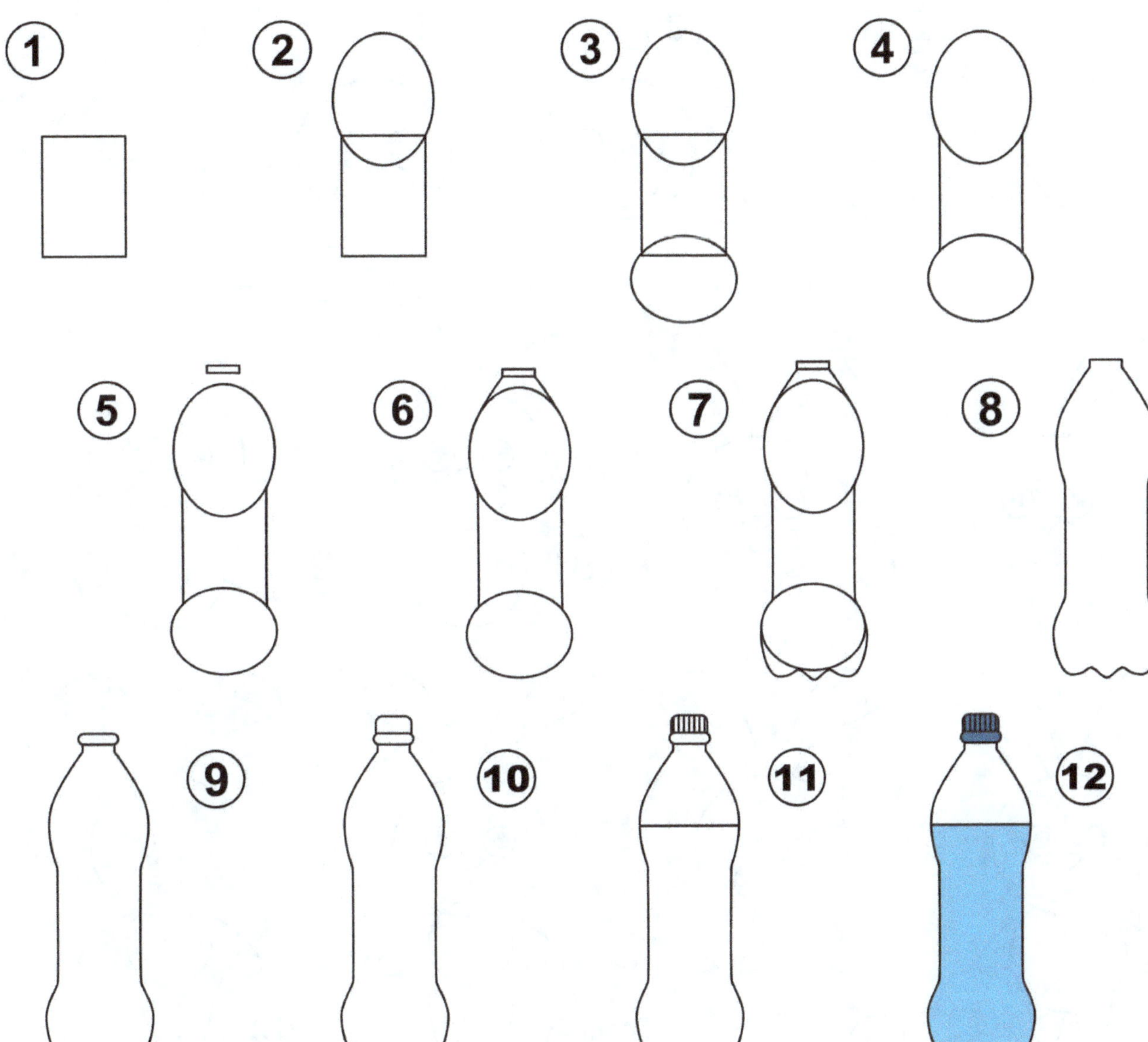

Bunny

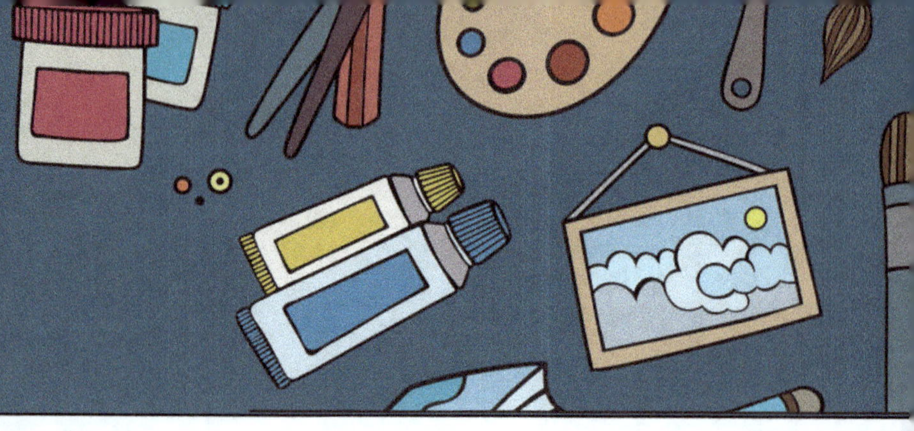

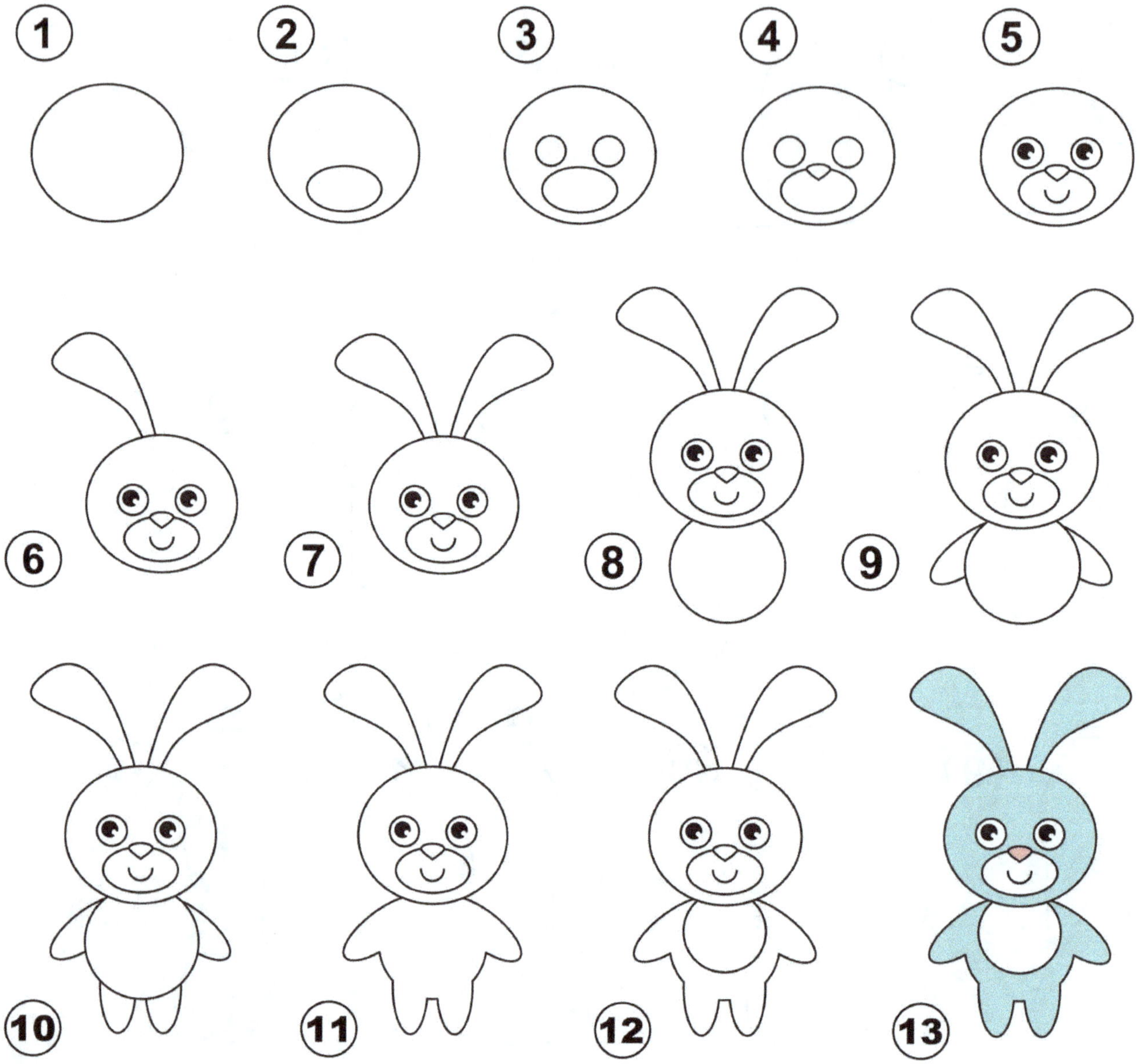

Butterfly

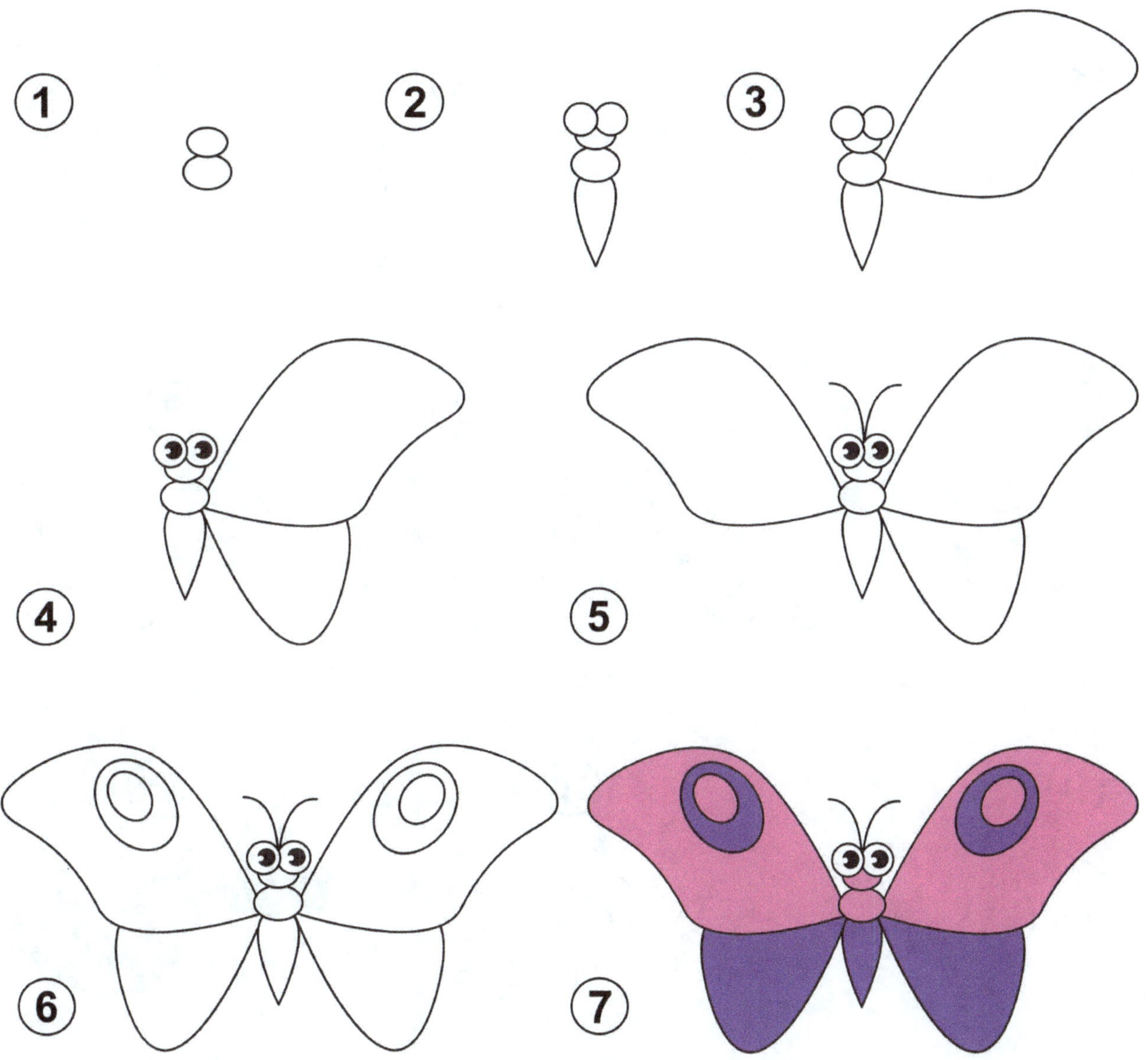

Caterpillar

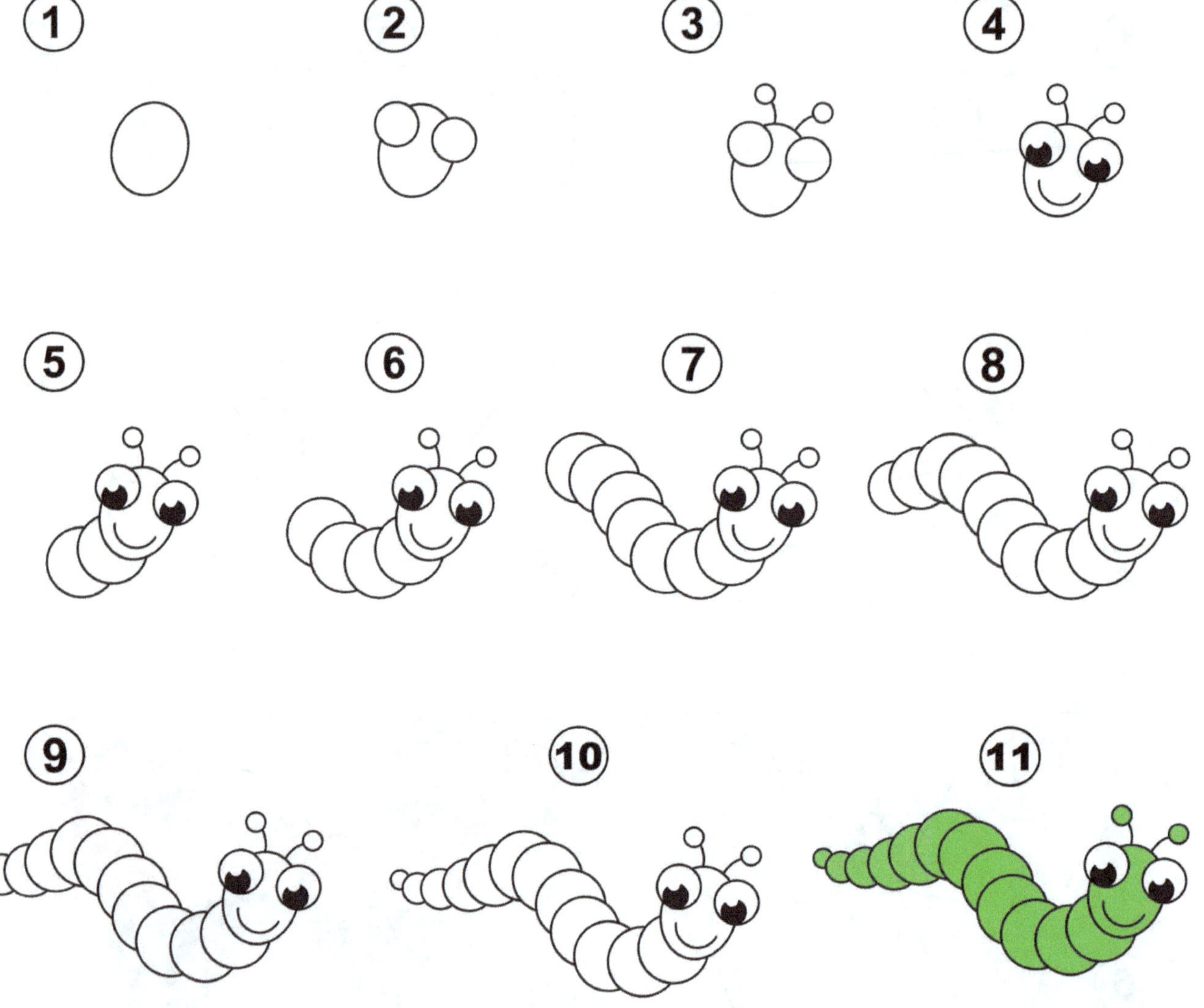

Cherry

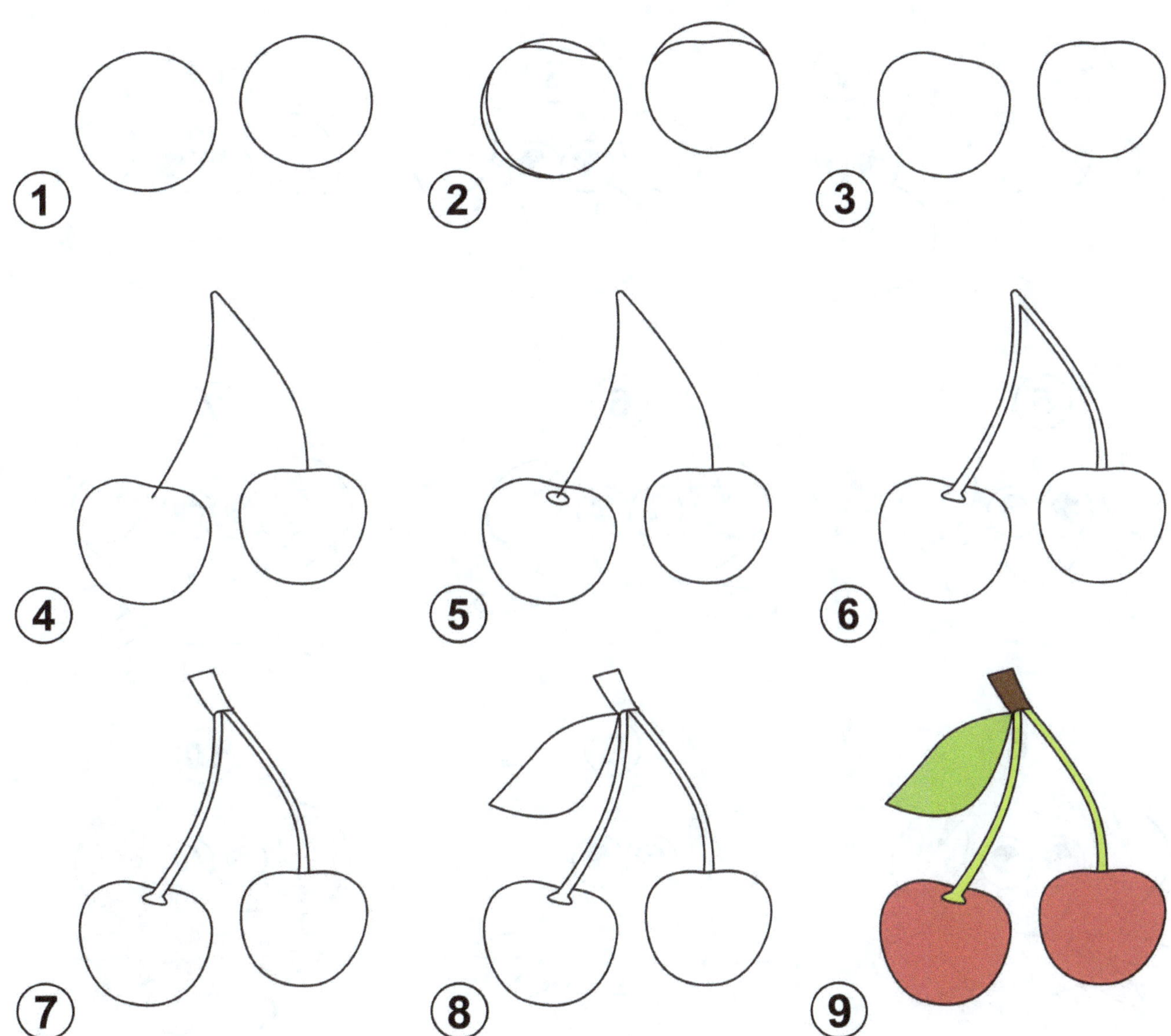

Crab

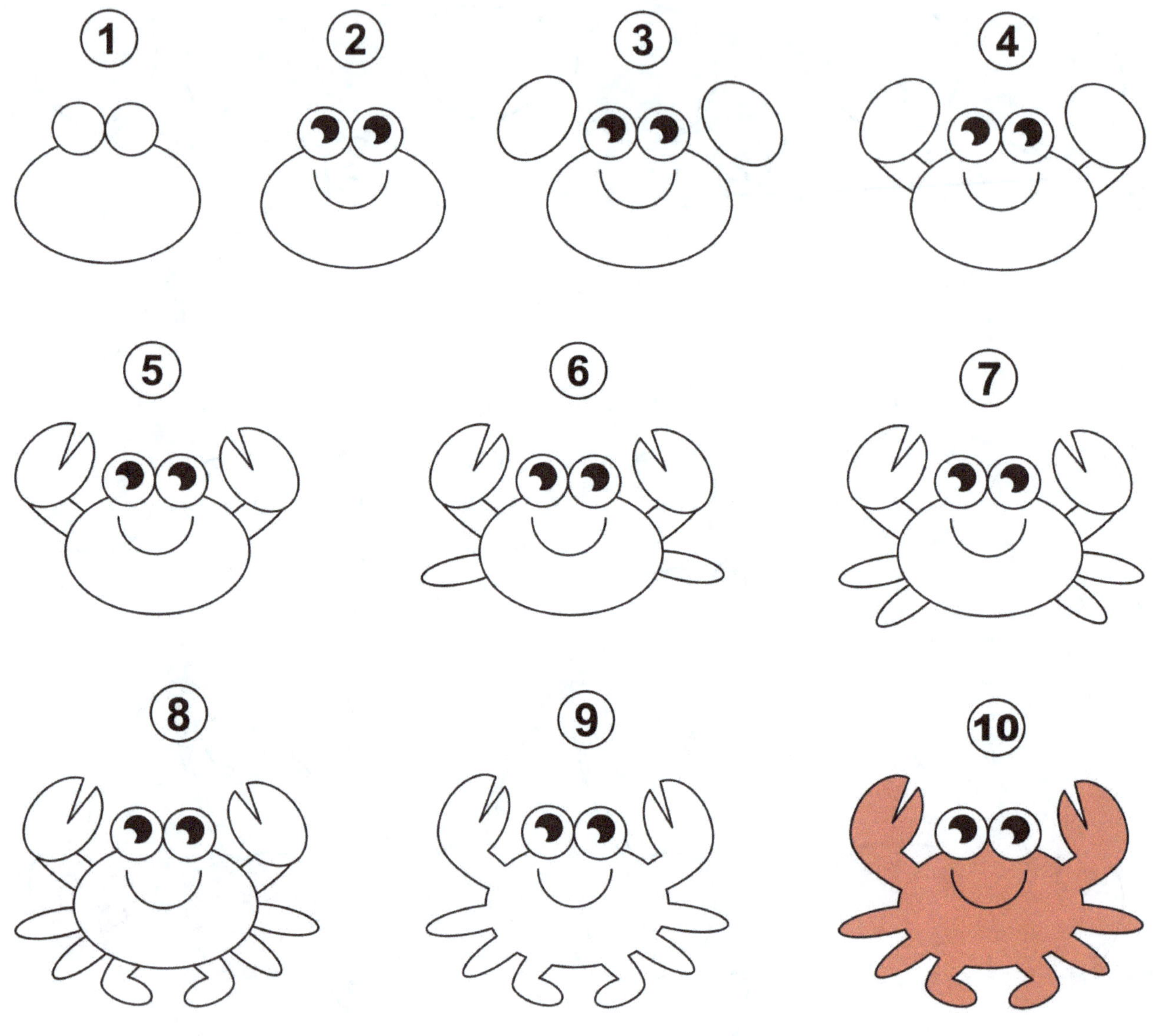

Crayfish

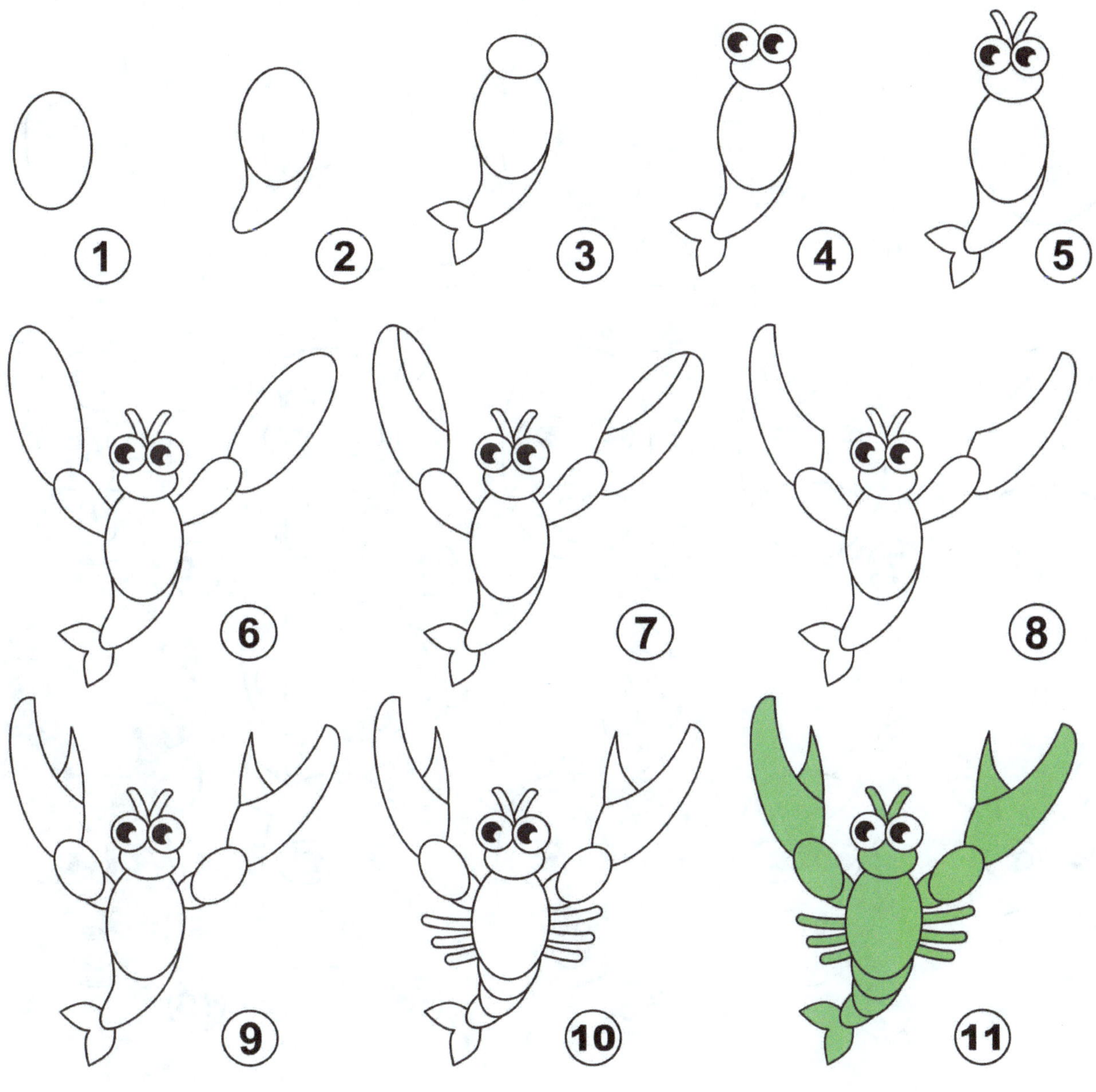

Deer head

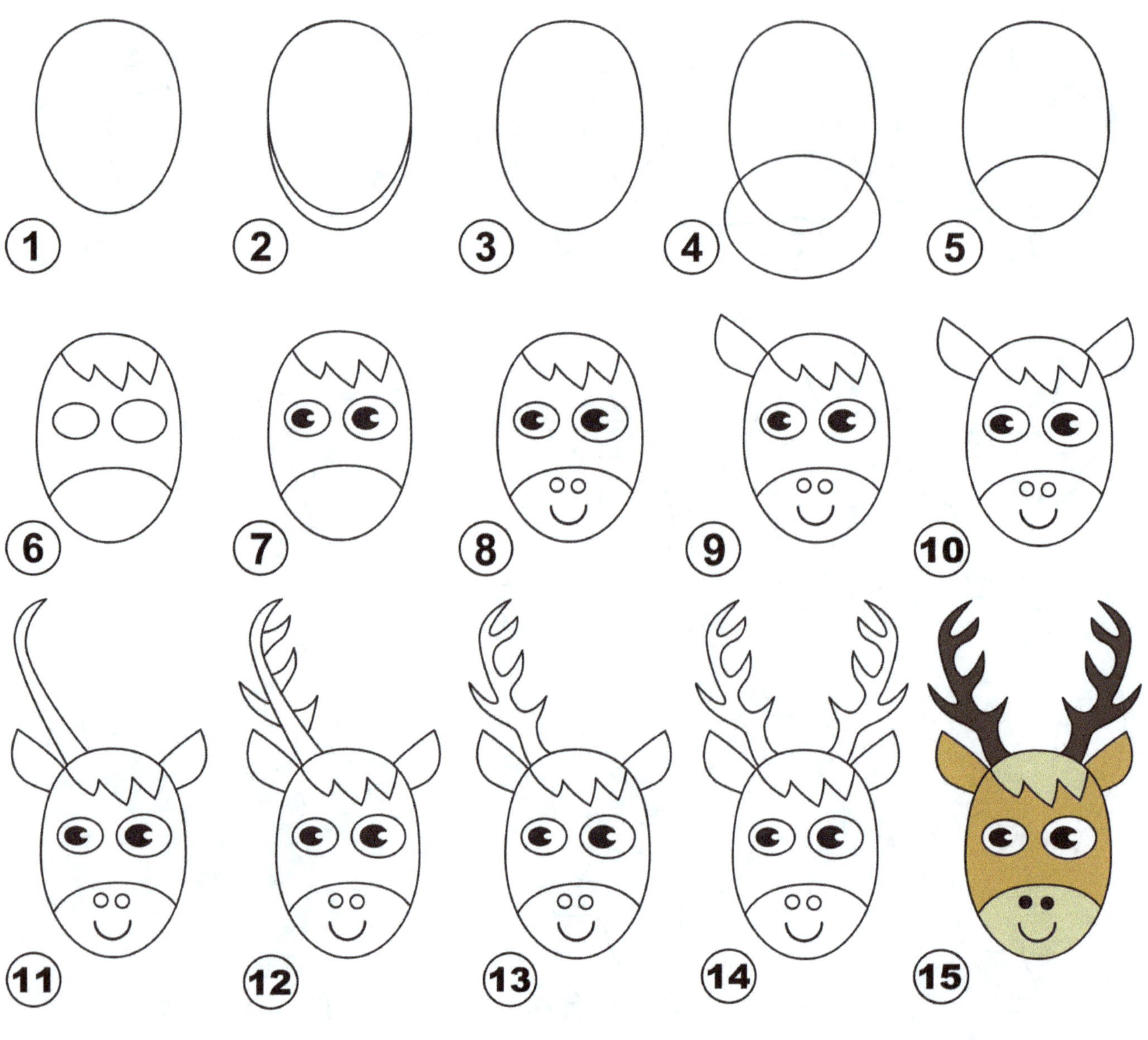

Dolphin

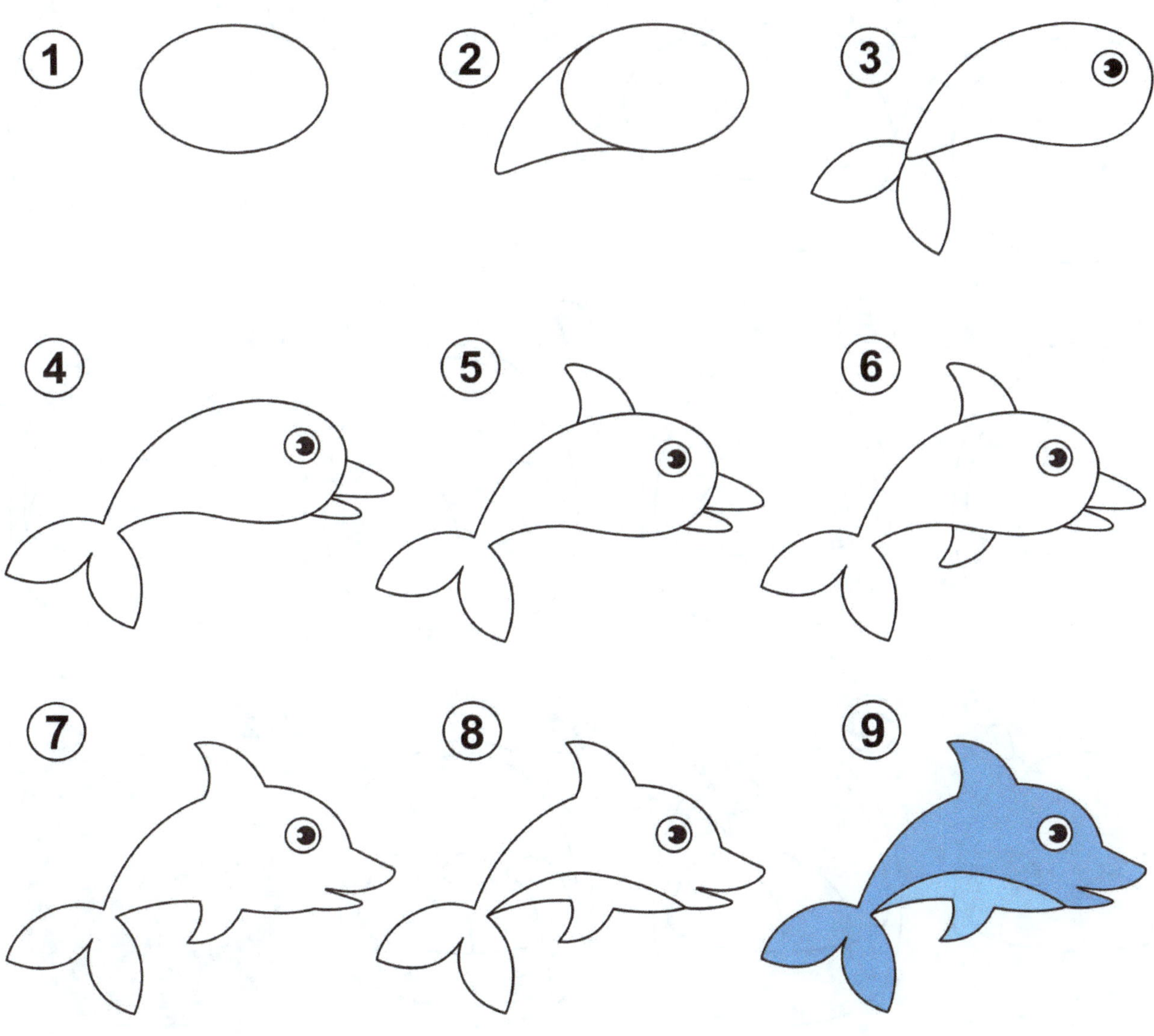

Easter
Basket

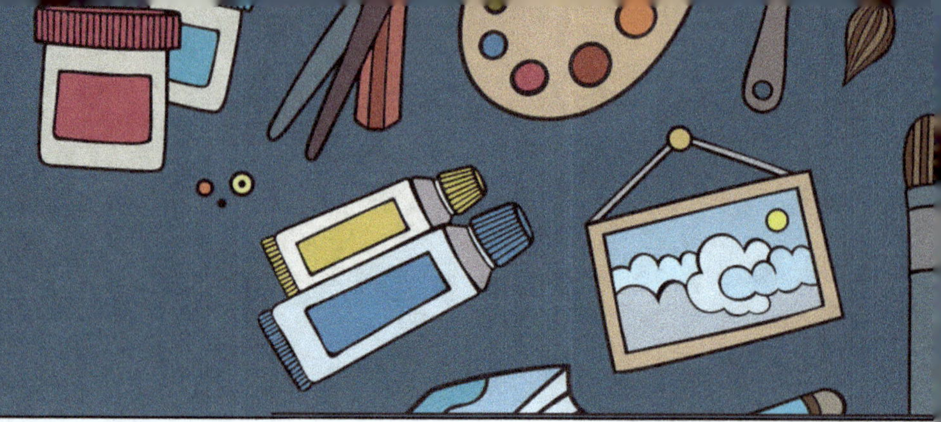

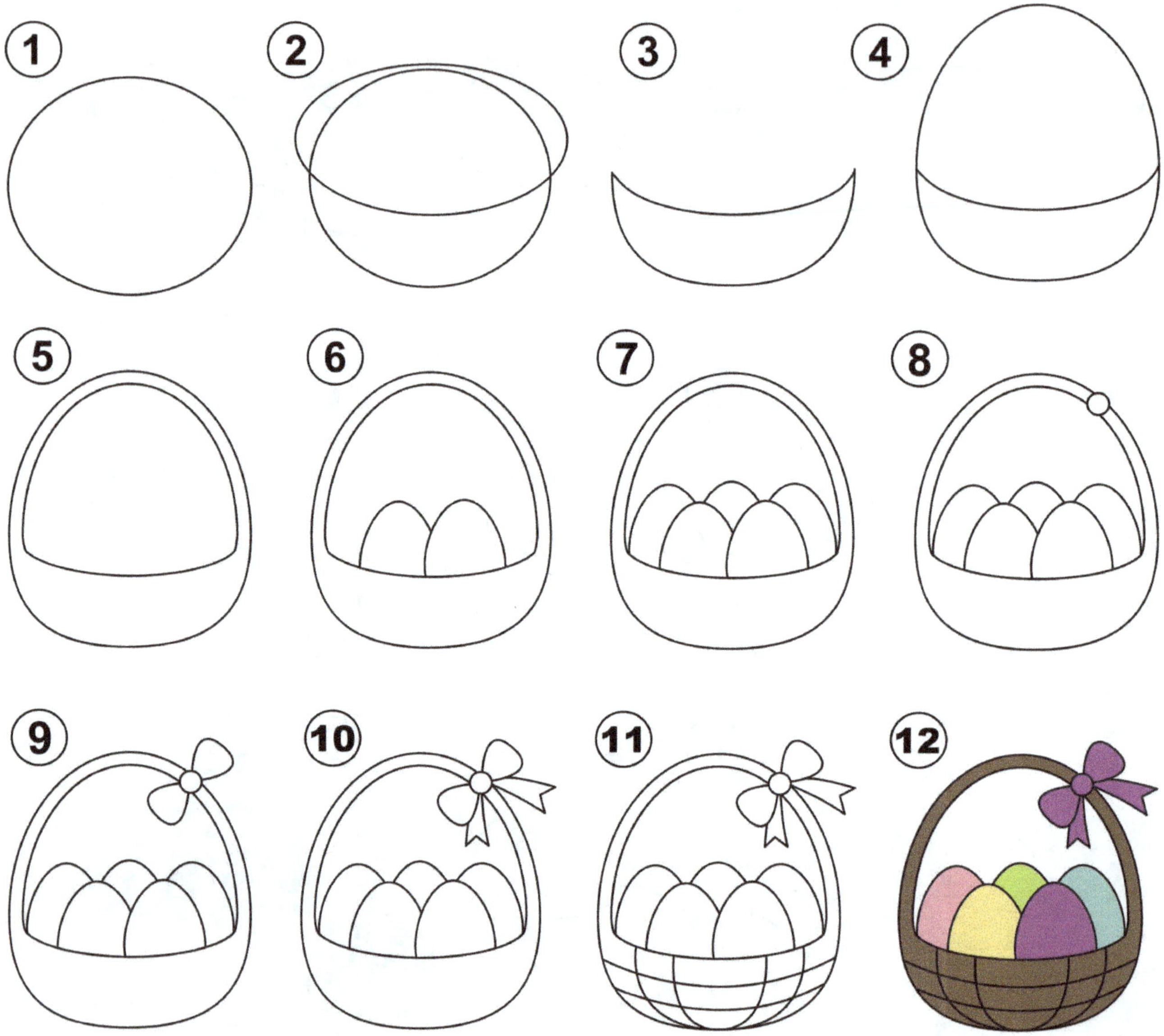

Elephant

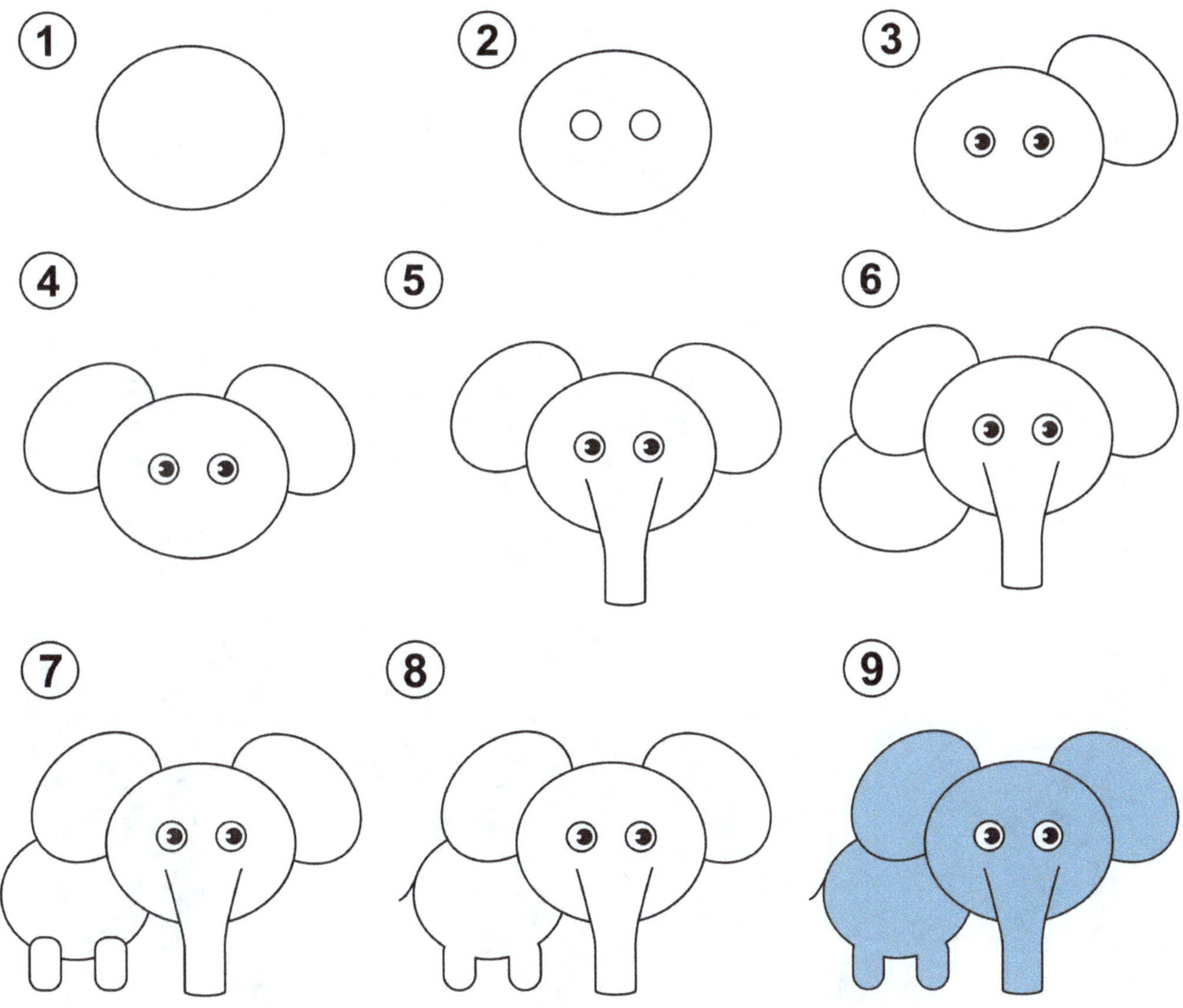

Elk

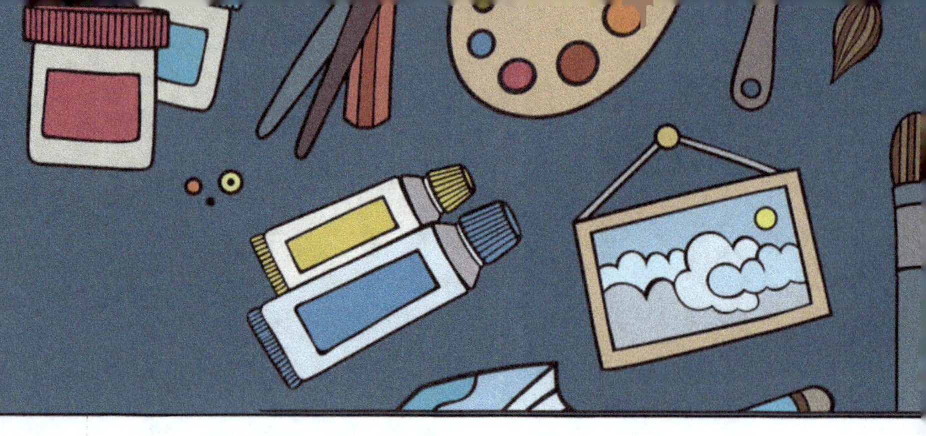

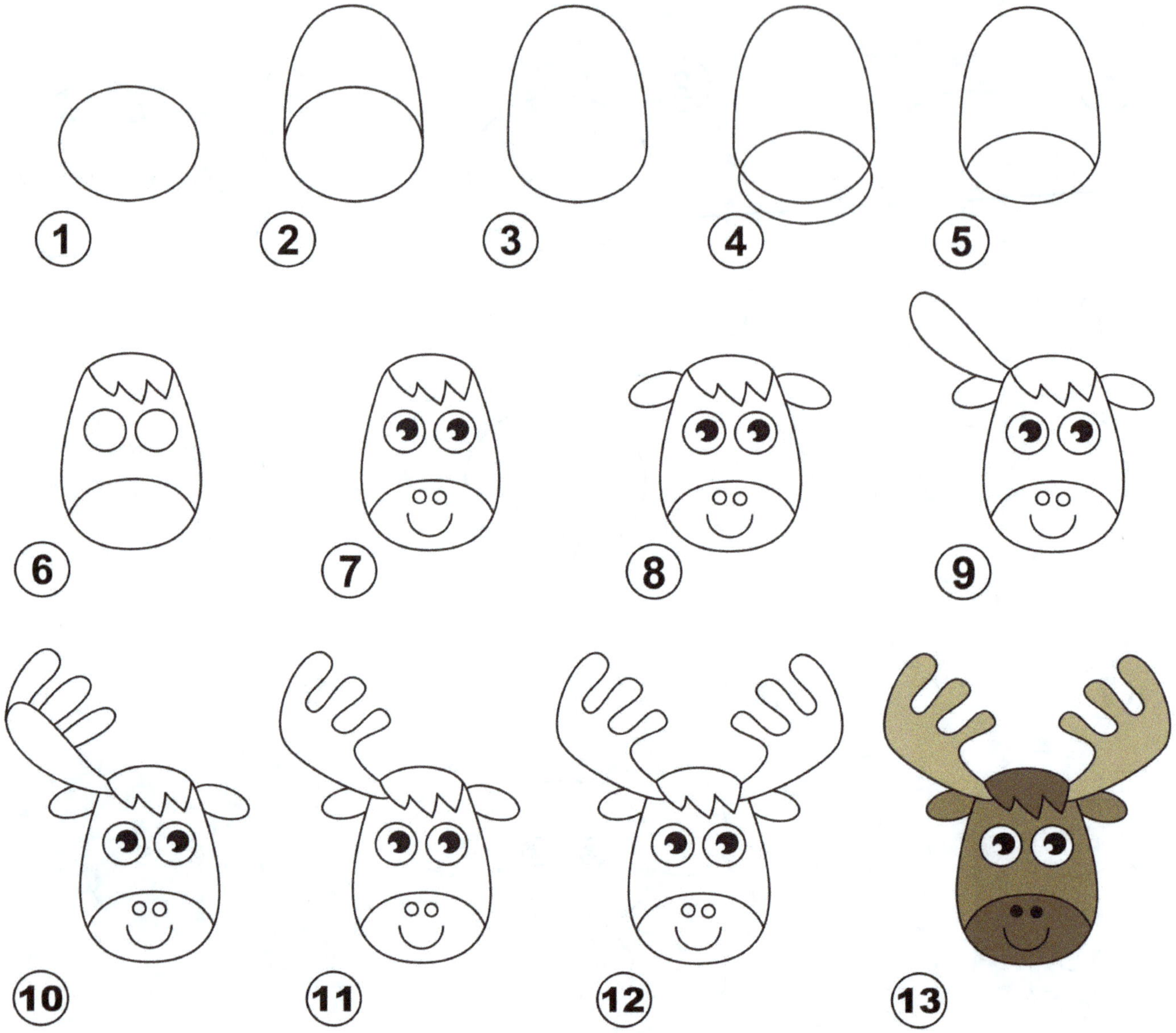

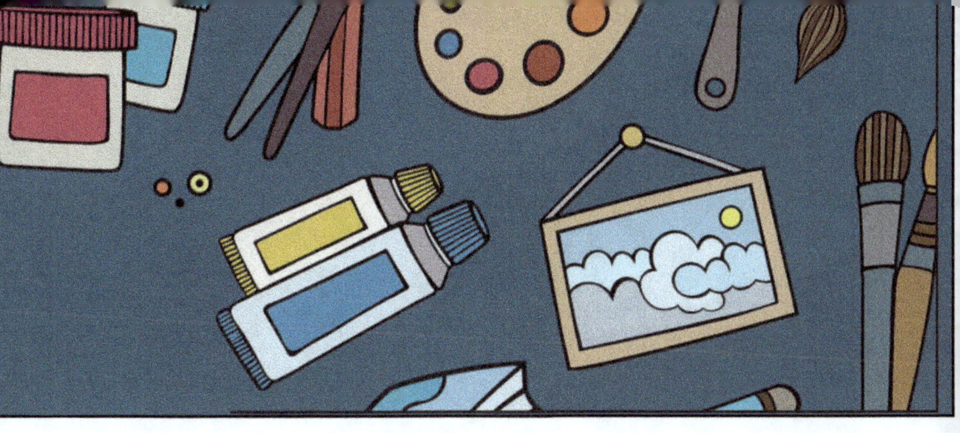

Fish

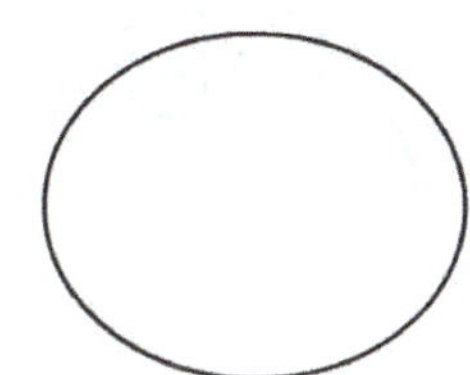

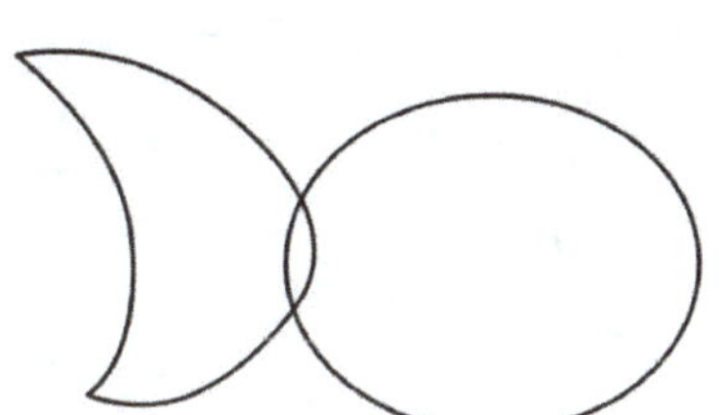

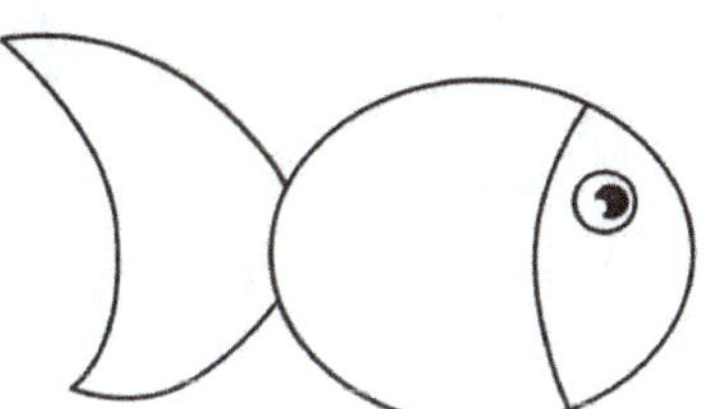

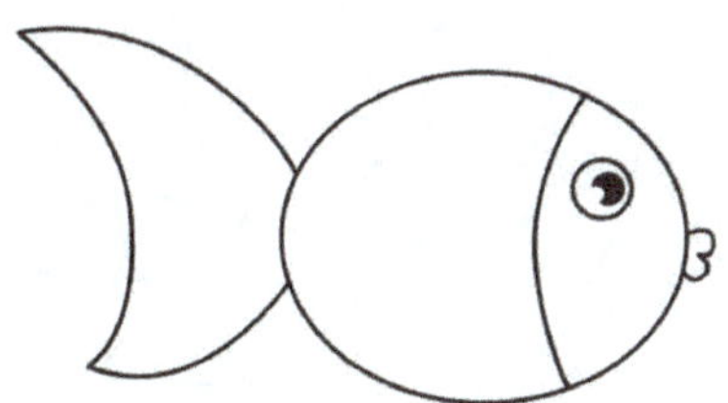

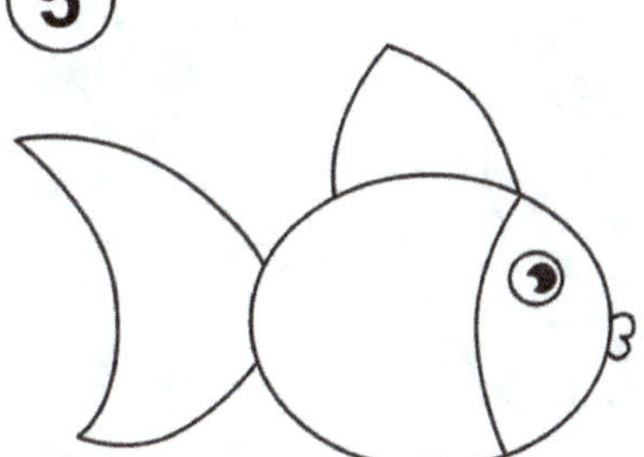

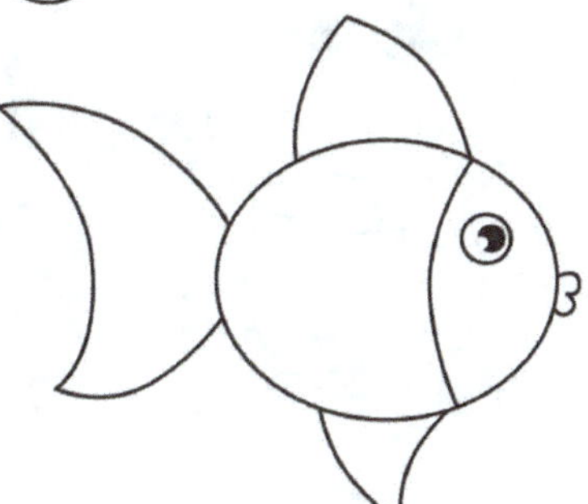

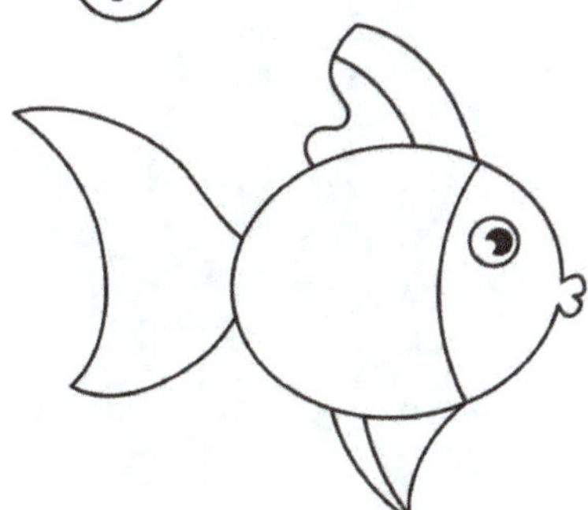

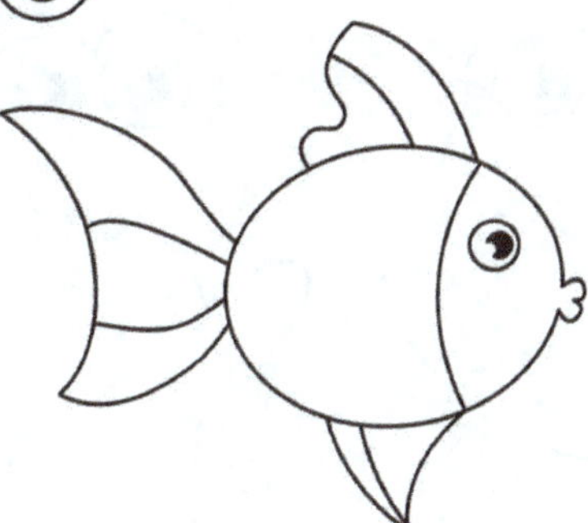

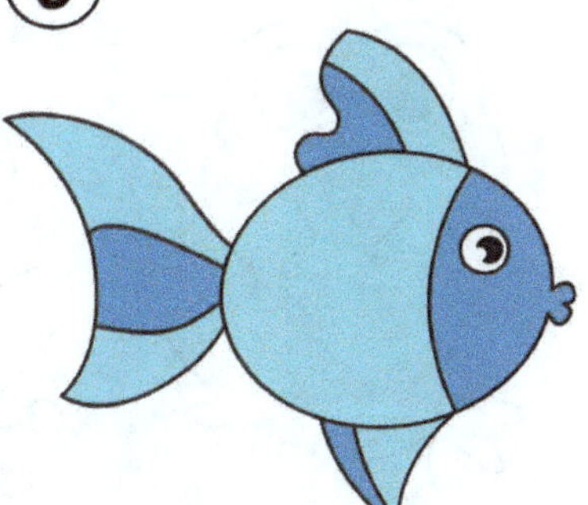

Frog

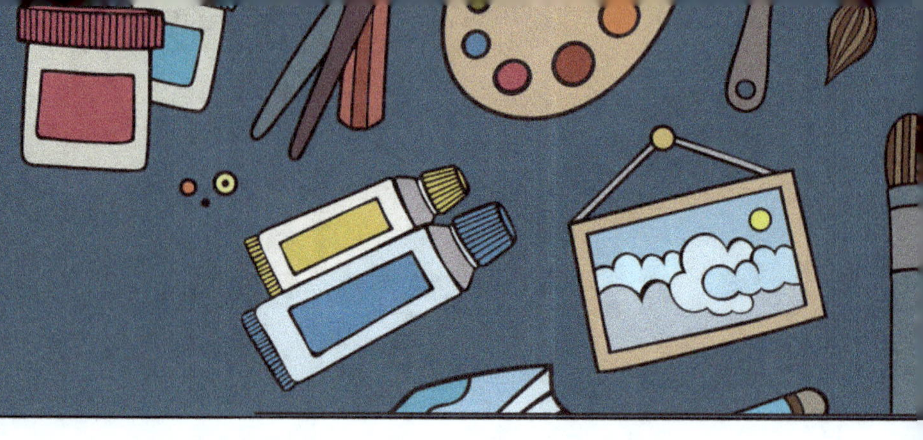

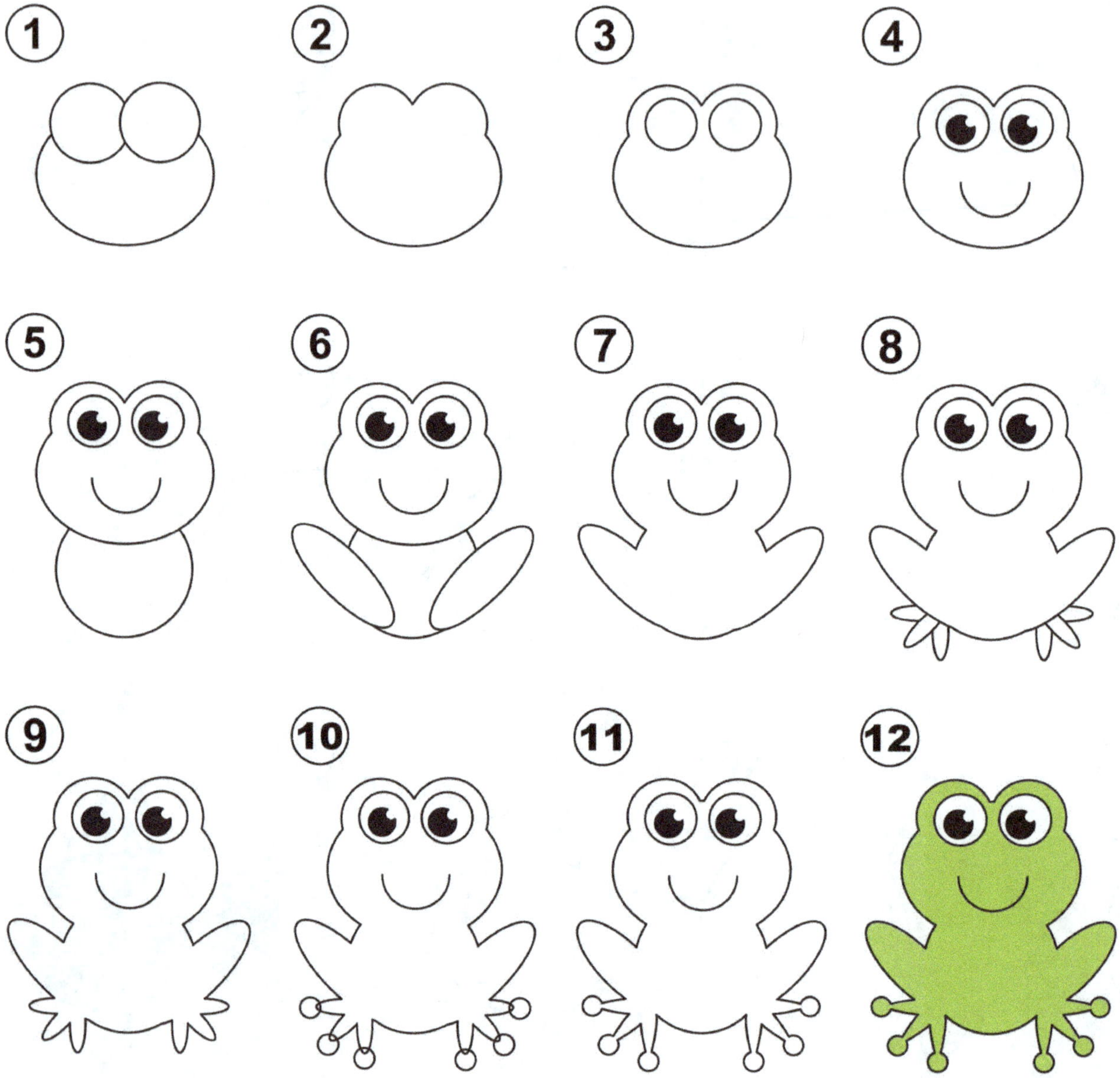

Funny Fish

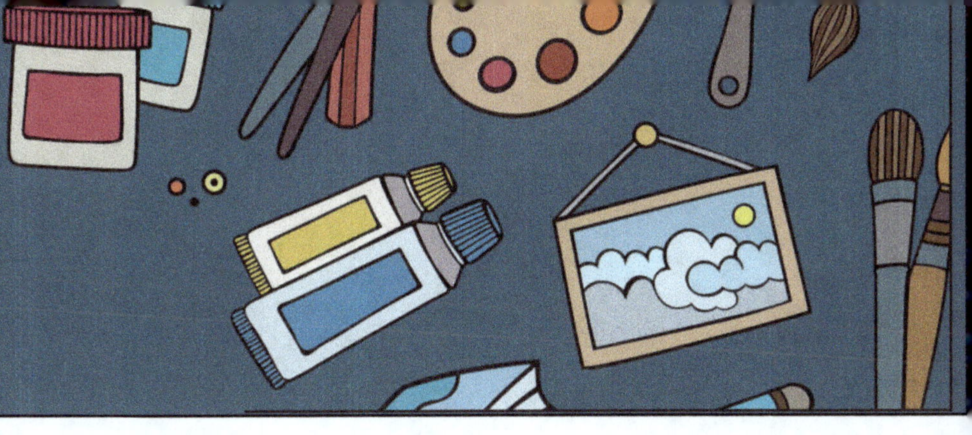

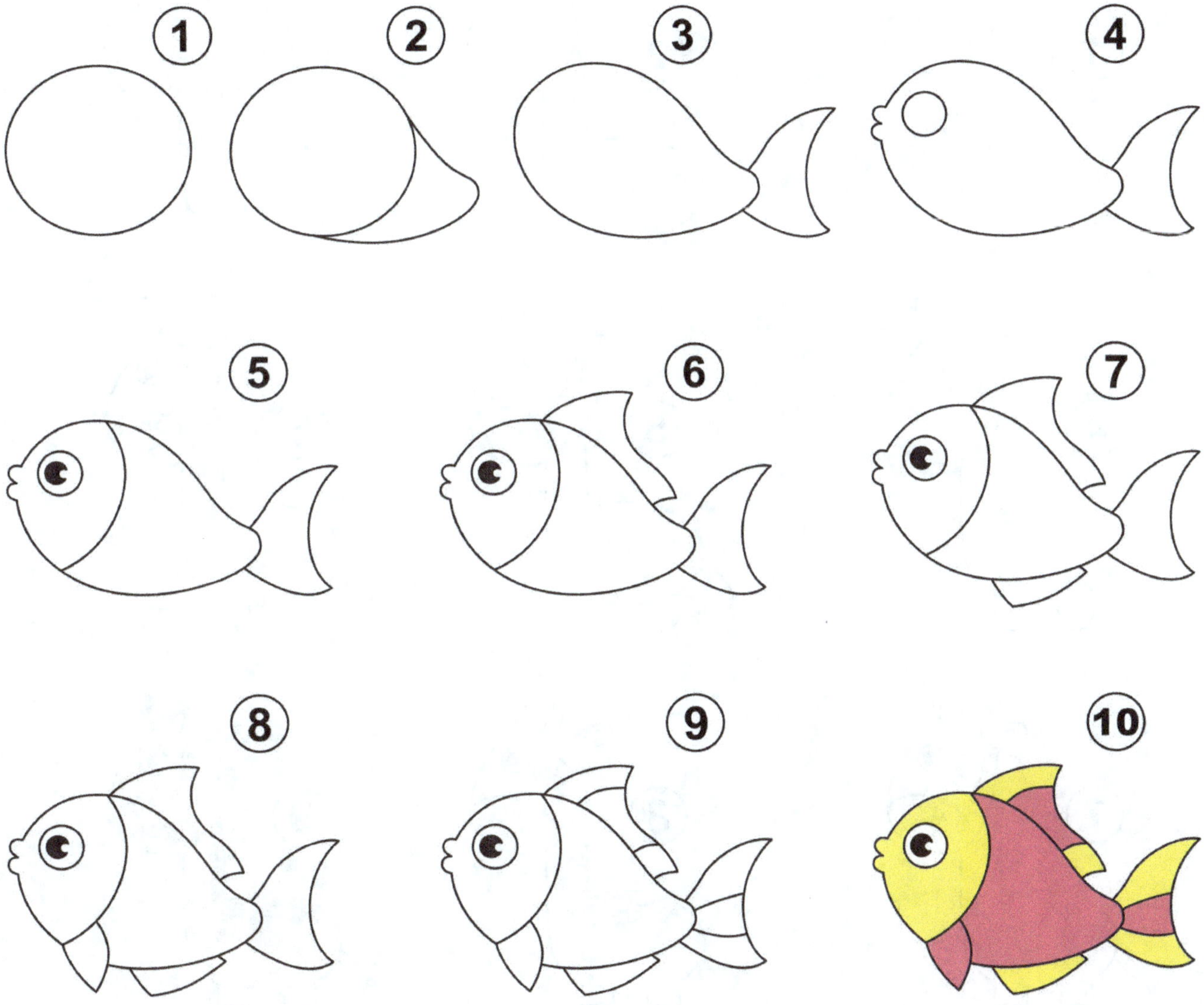

Giraffe

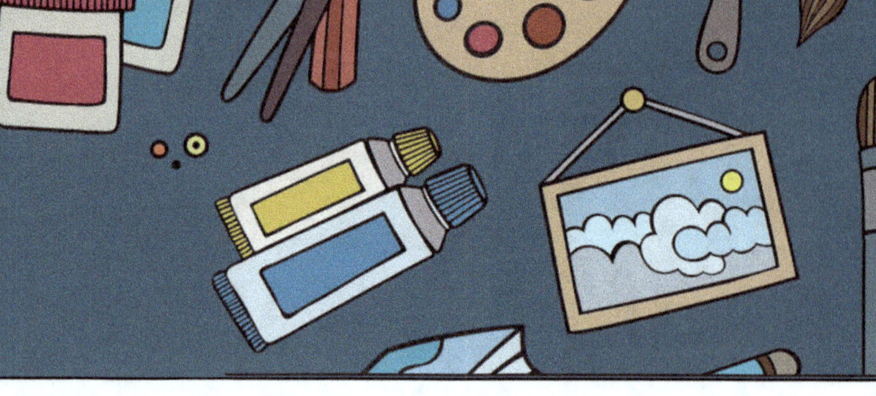

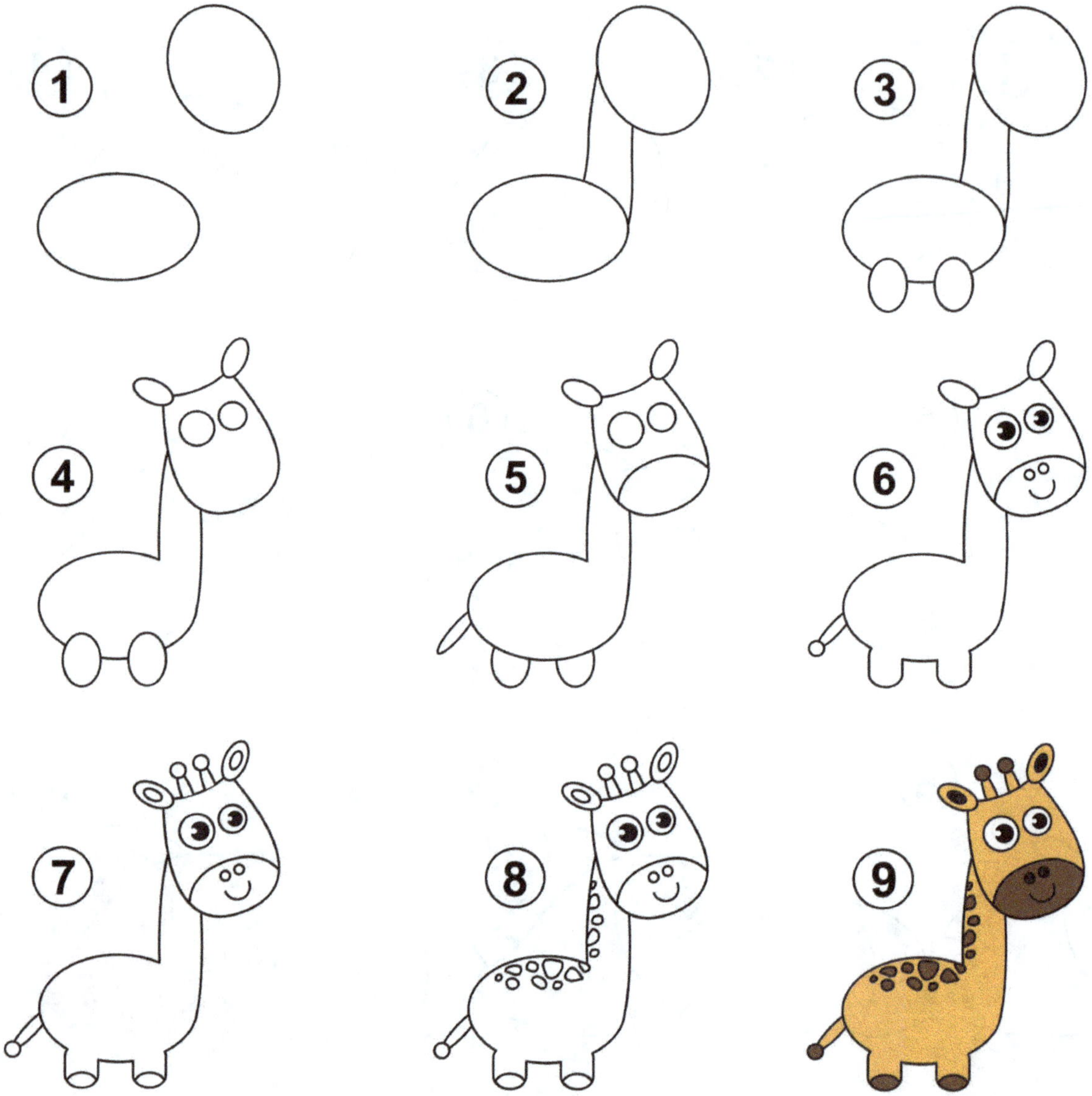

Globe

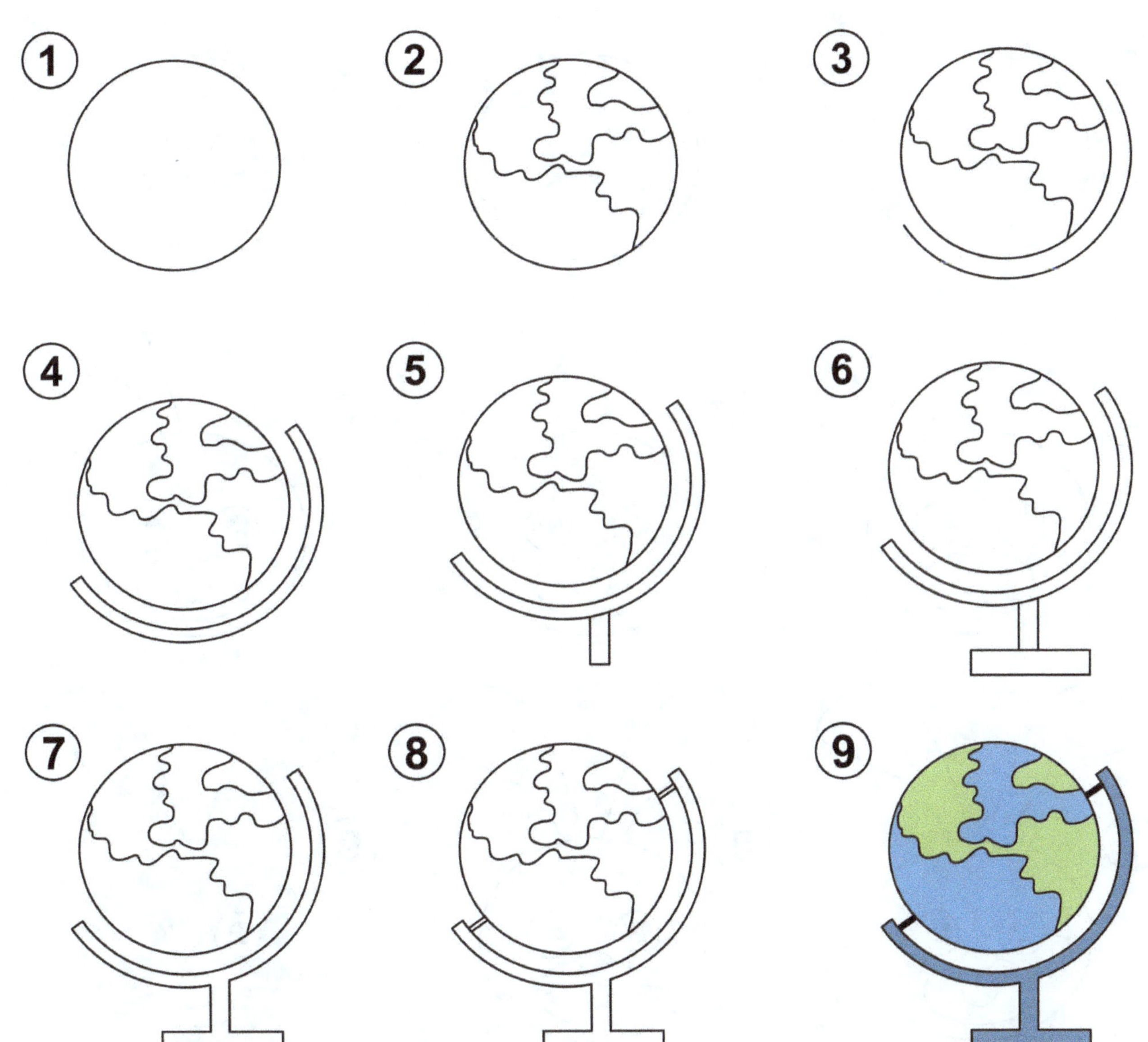

Hare Head

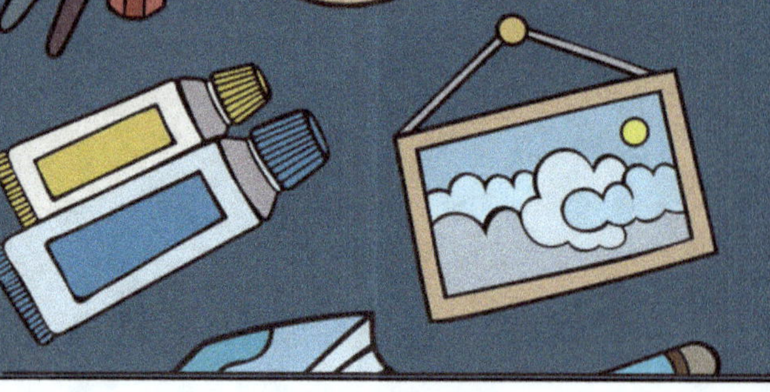

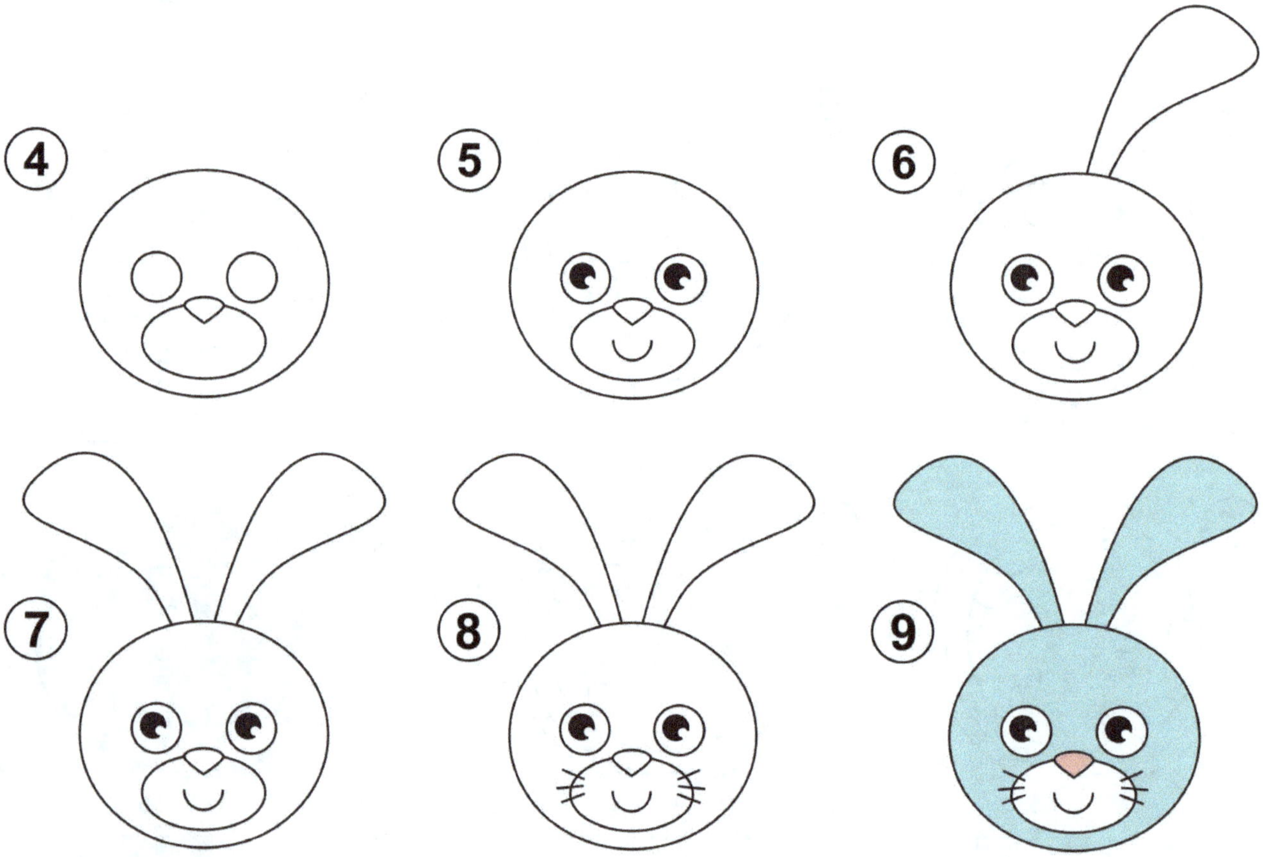

Heart

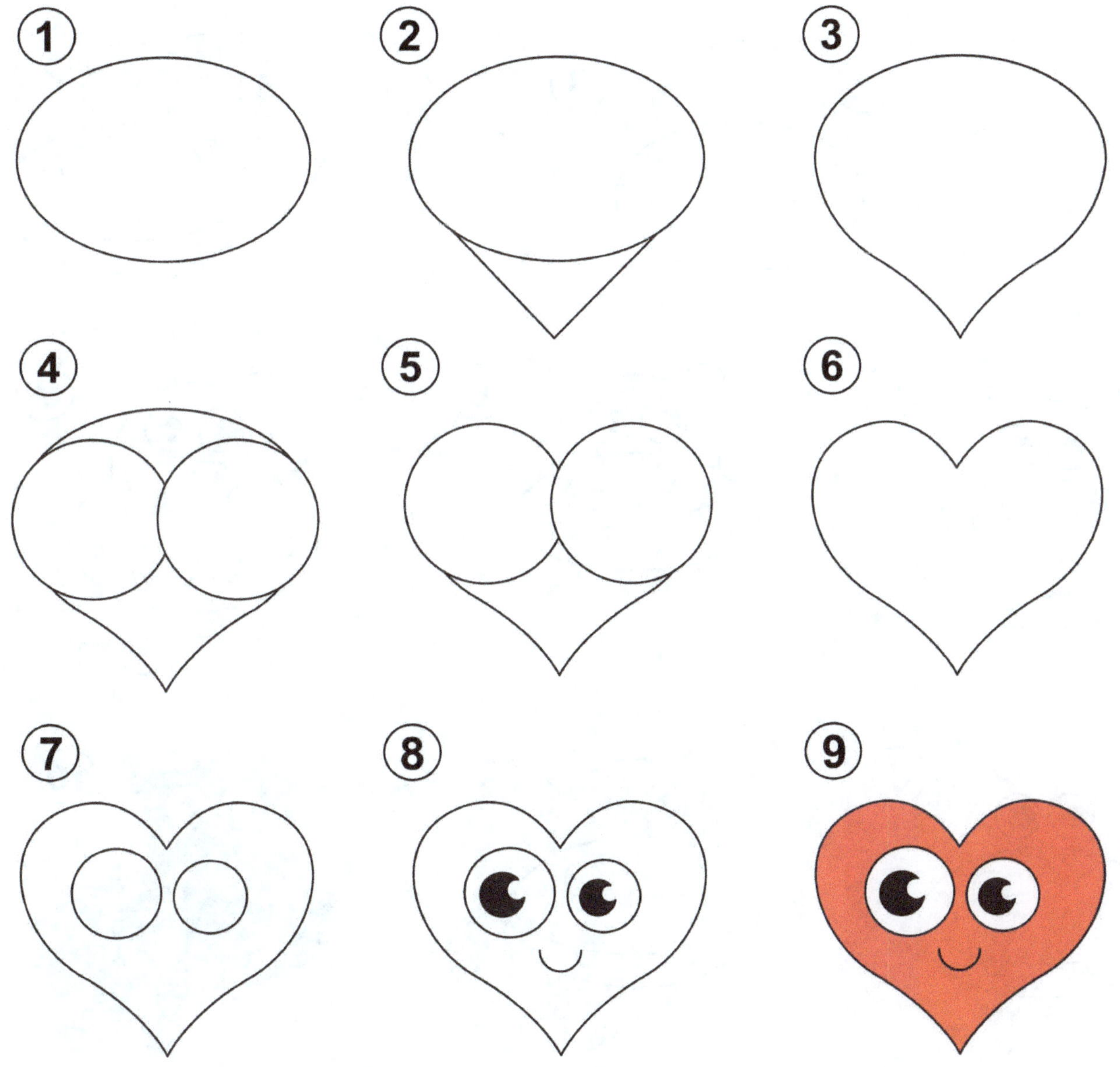

Hippo

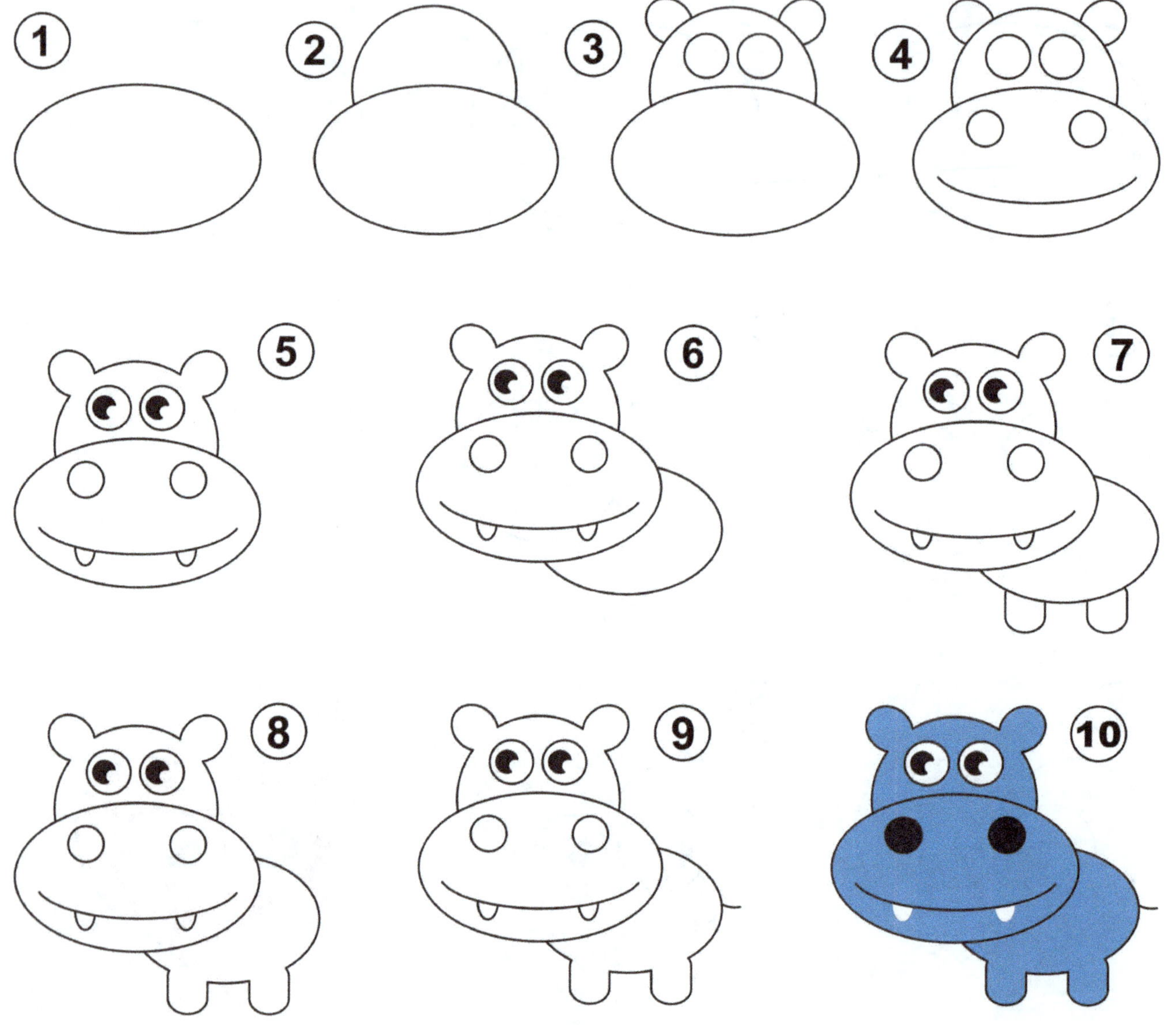

Horse

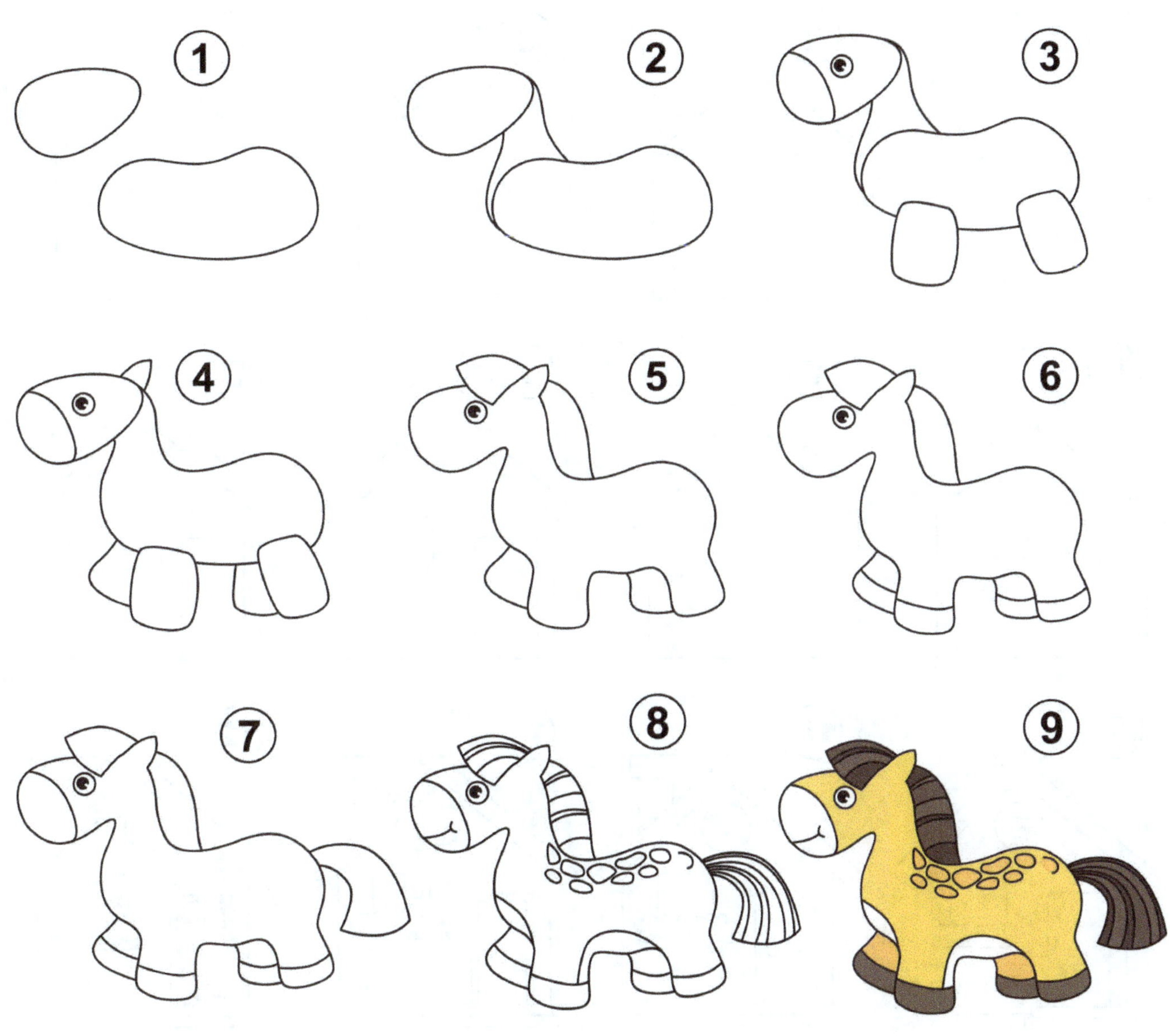

House

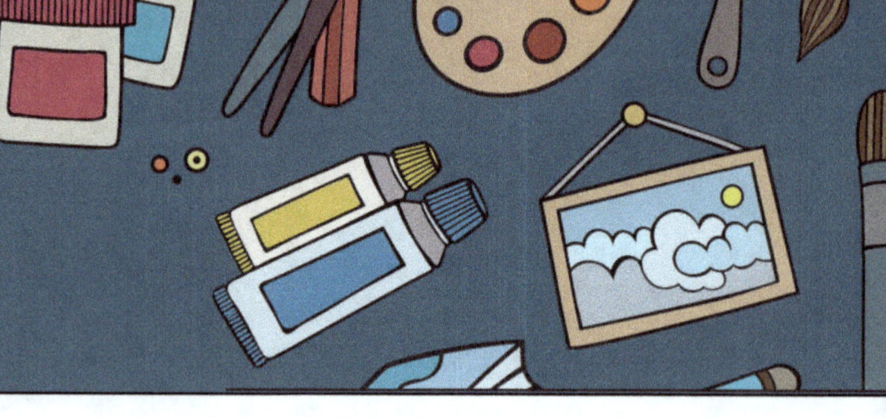

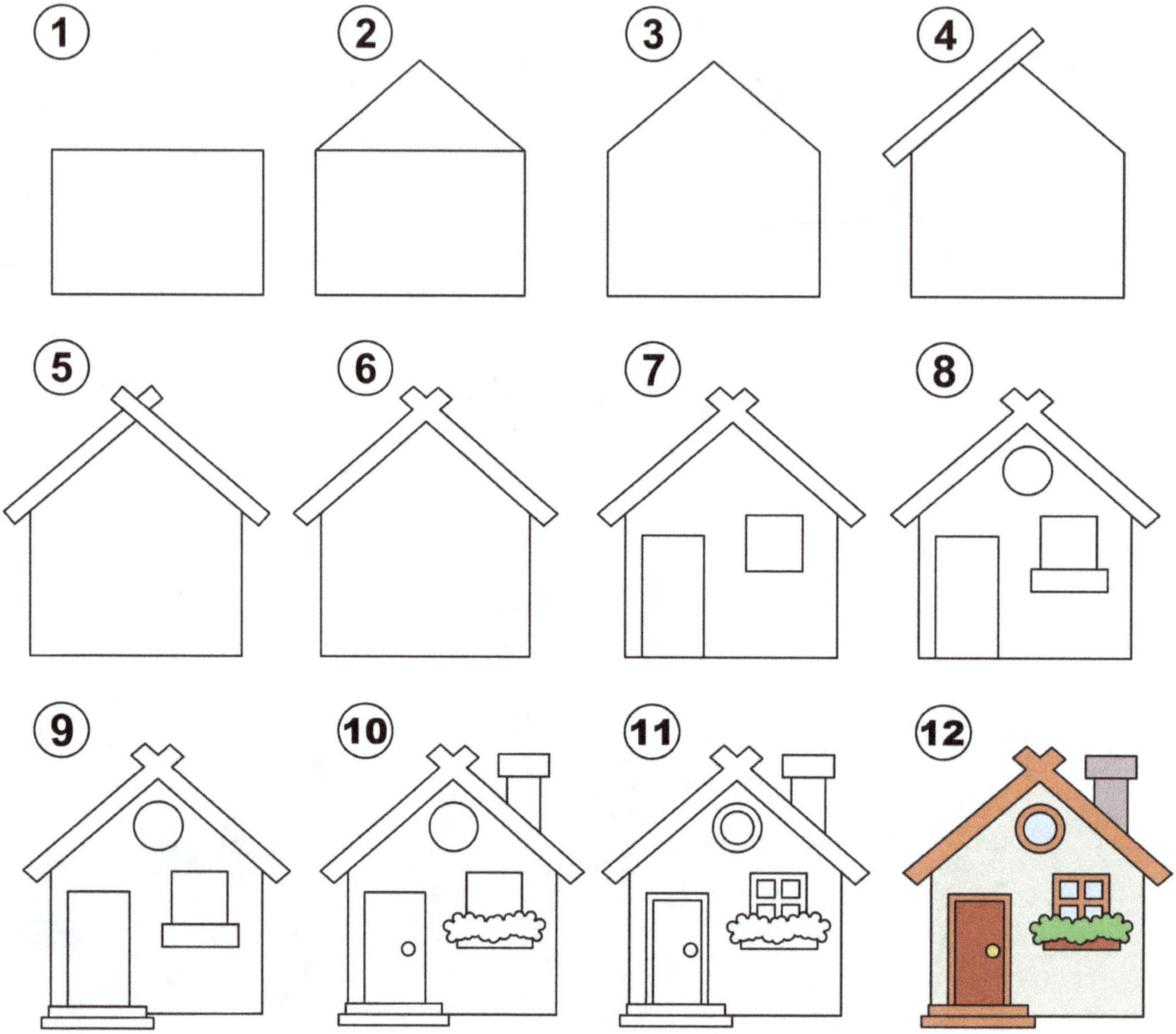

Ice cream

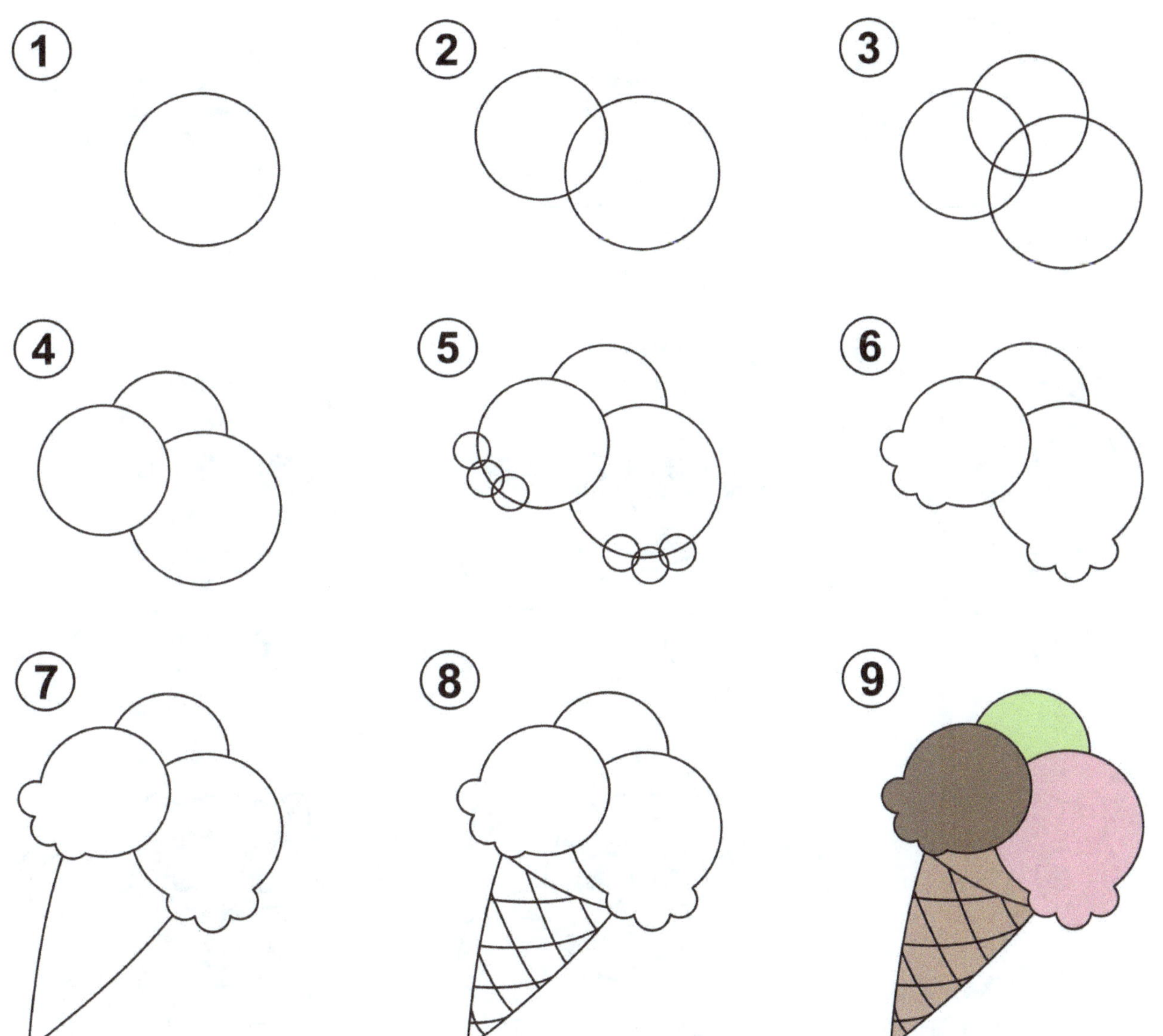

Kitten

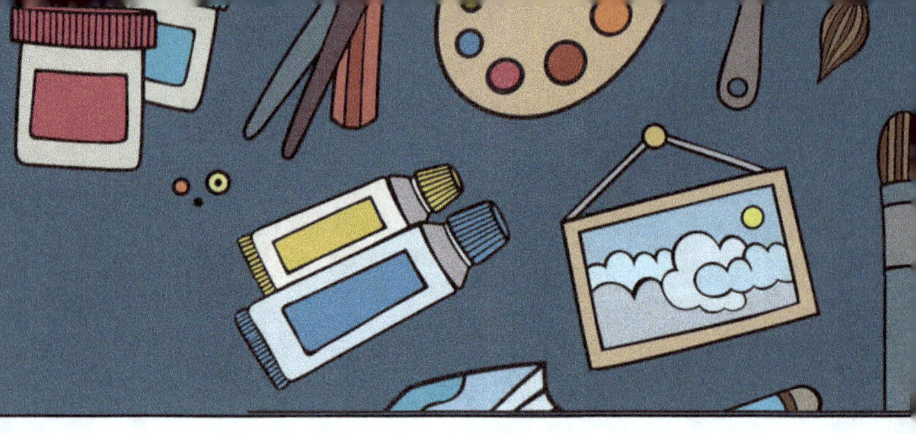

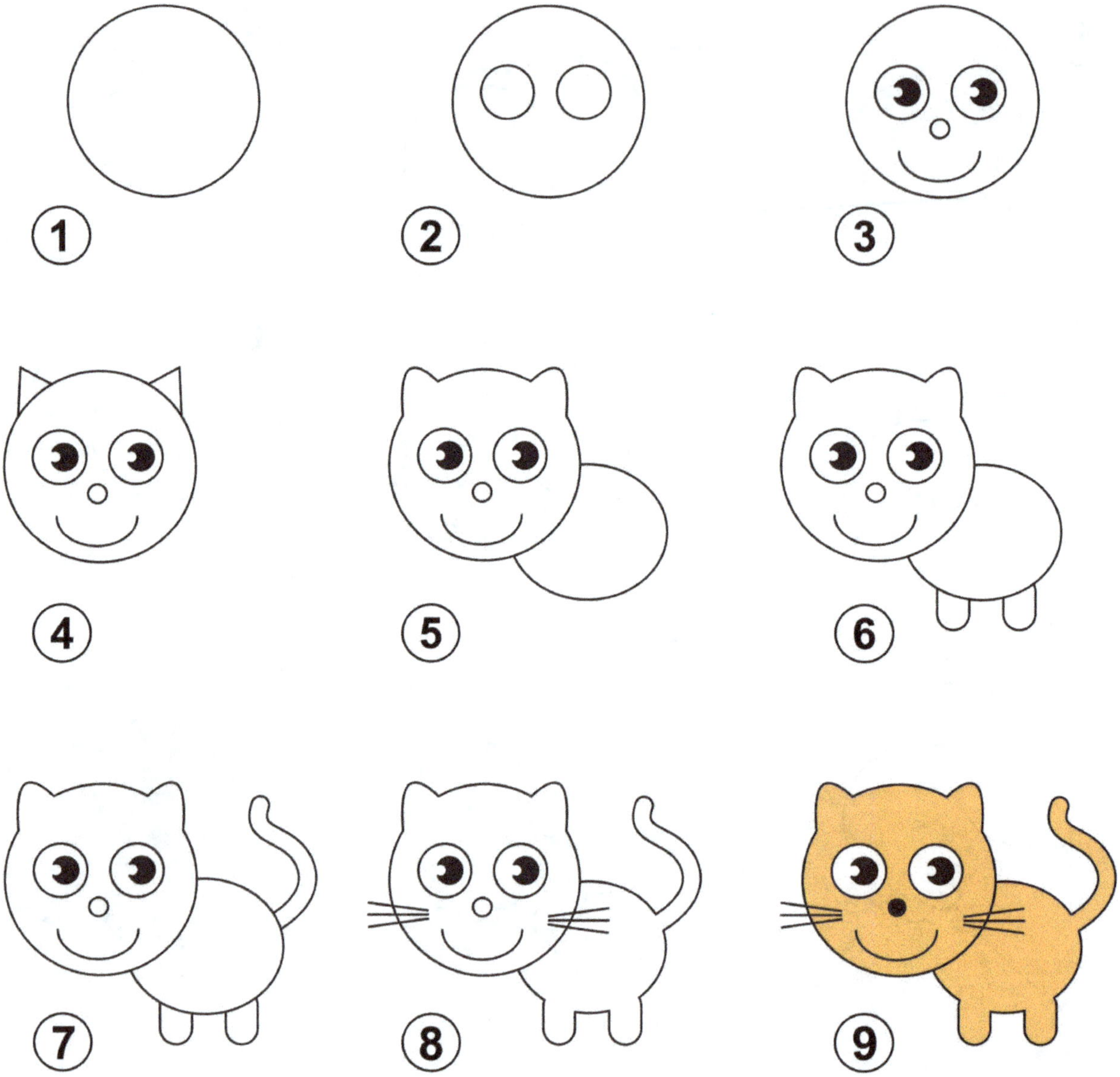

① ② ③

④ ⑤ ⑥

⑦ ⑧ ⑨

Ladybug

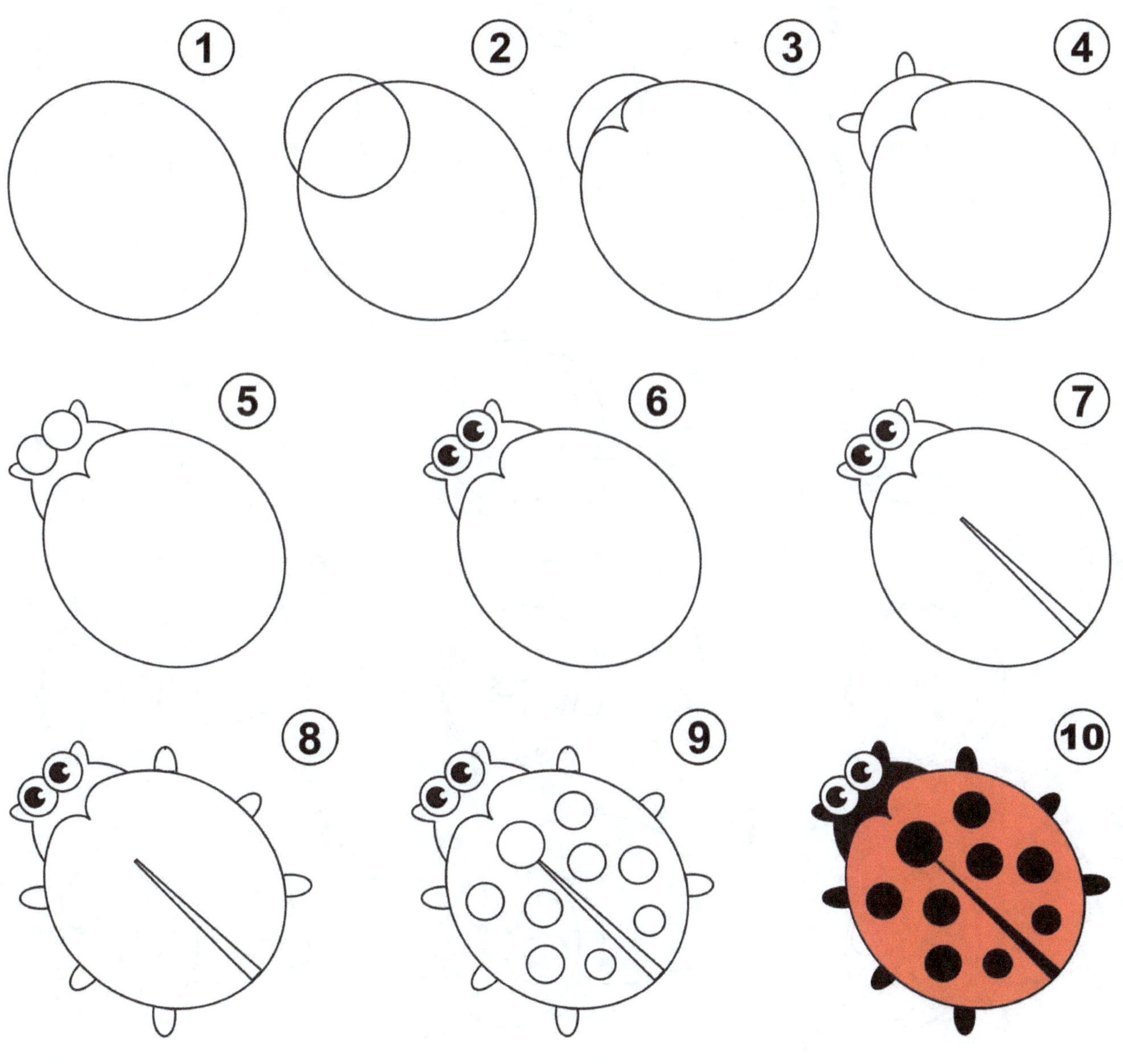

Lemon

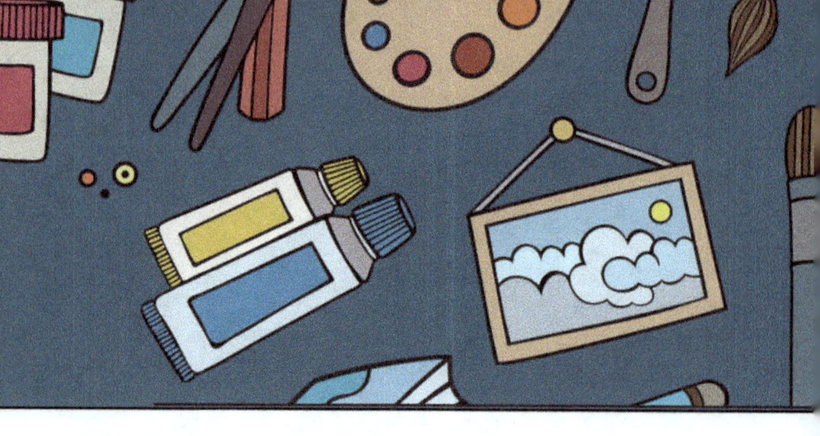

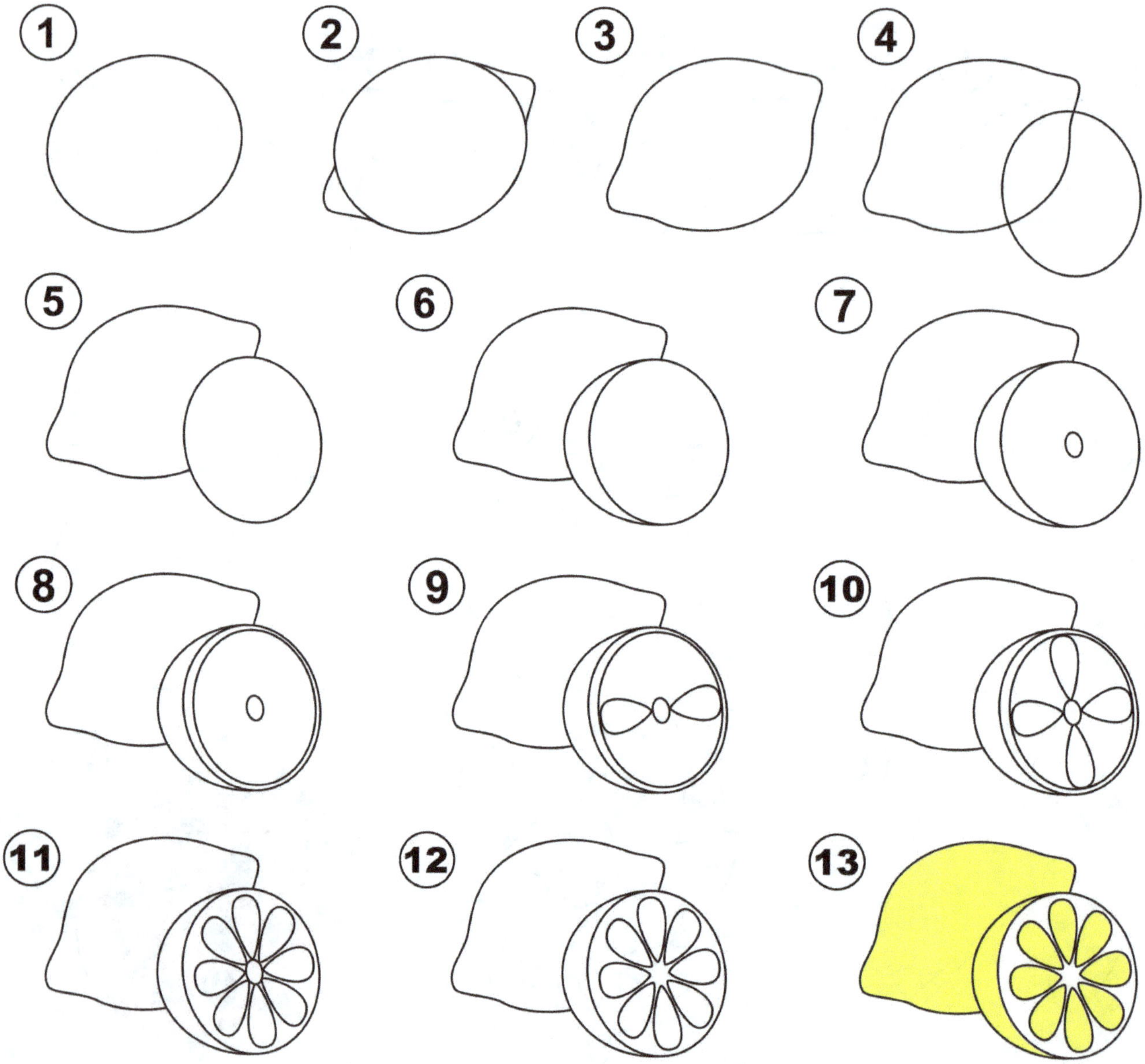

Monkey

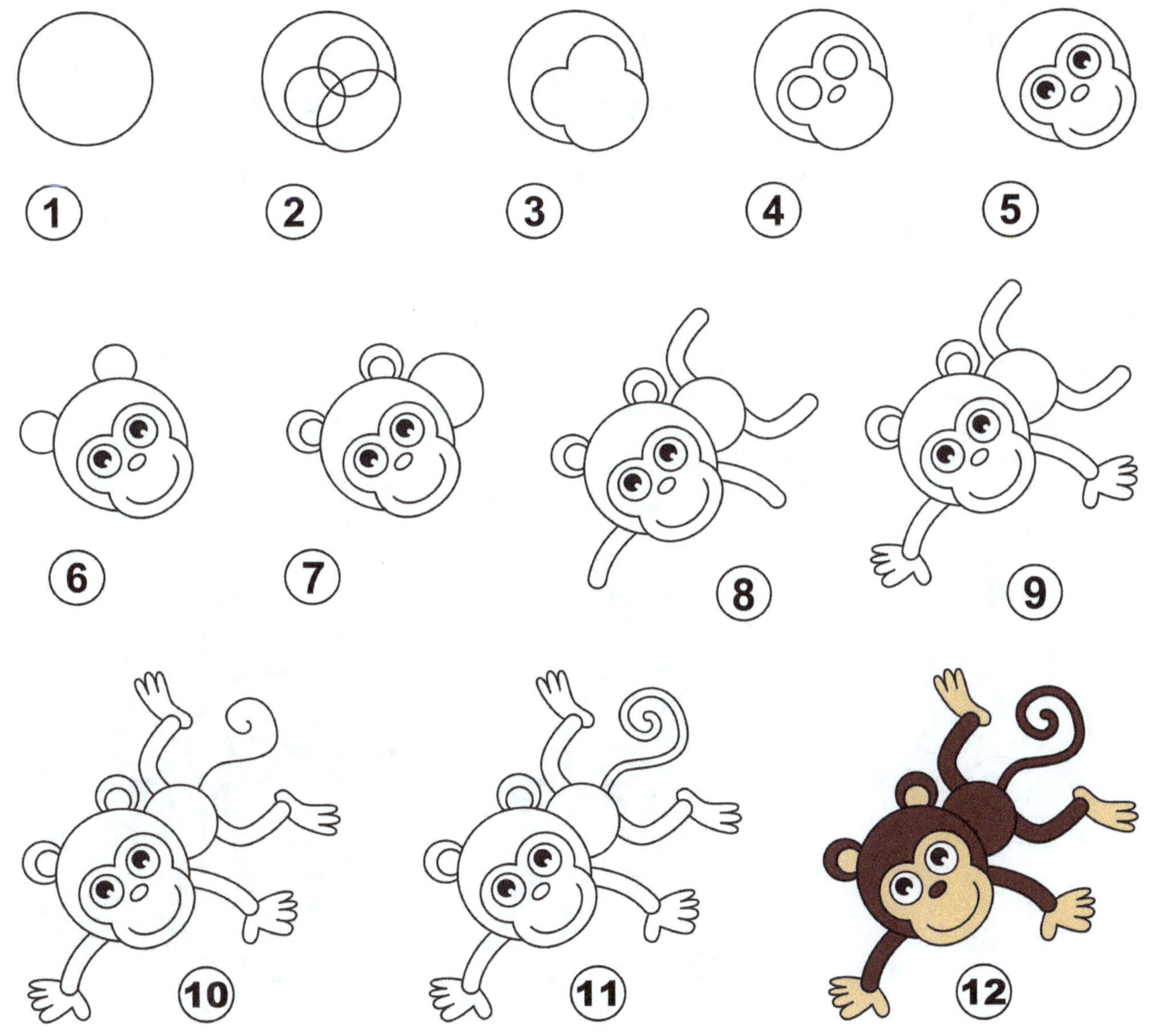

Moon

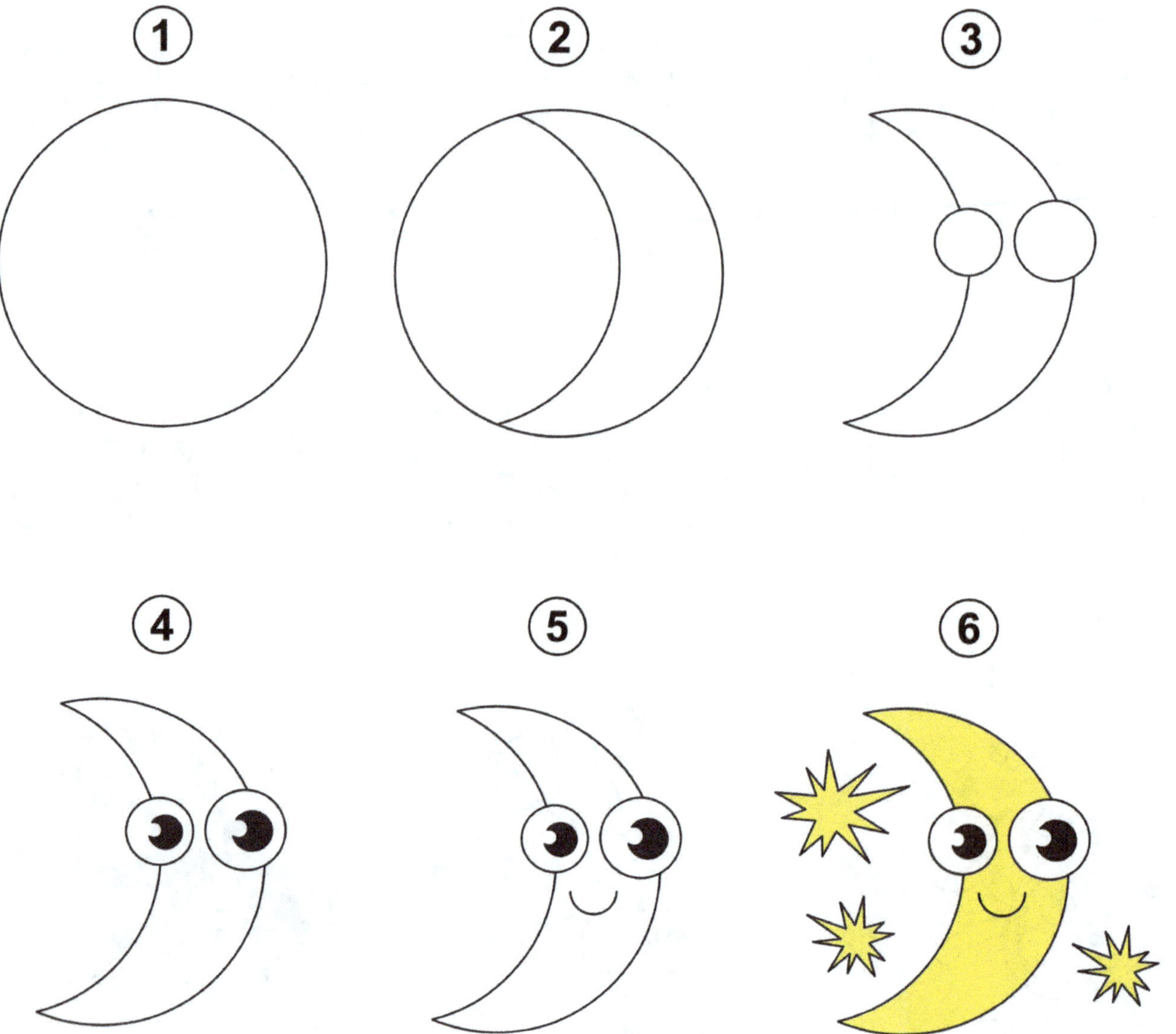

Mushroom

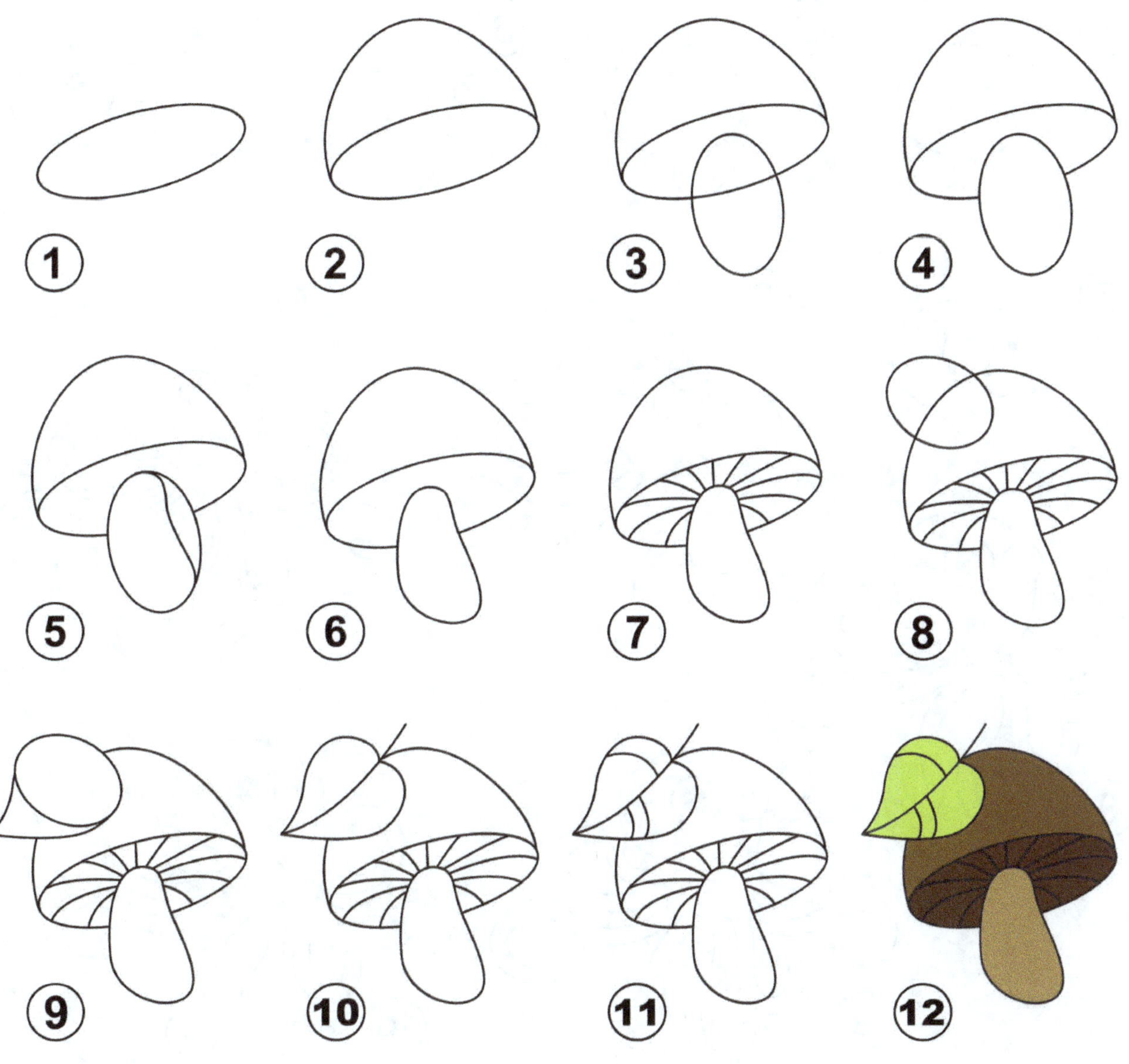

Octopus

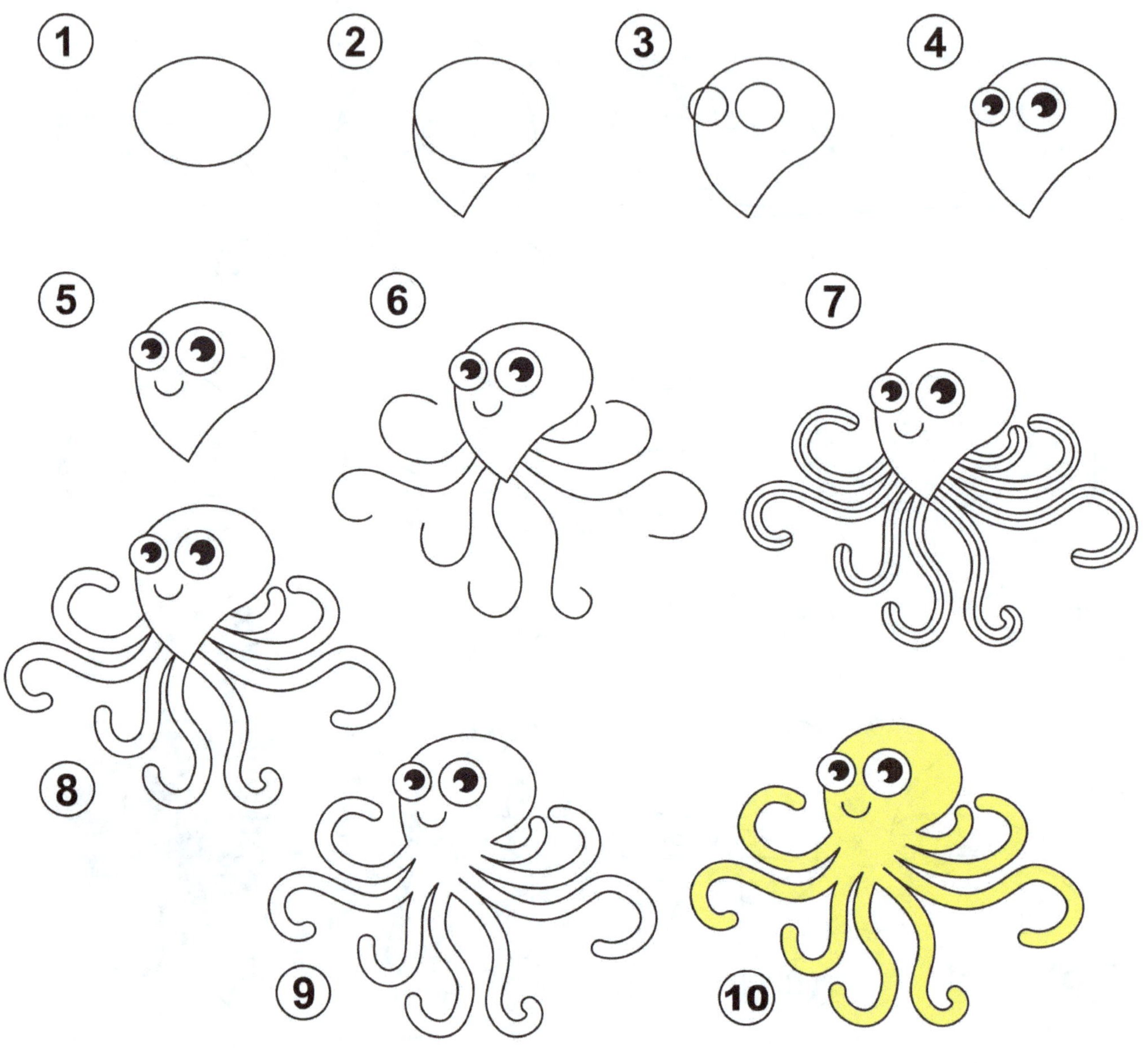

Owl

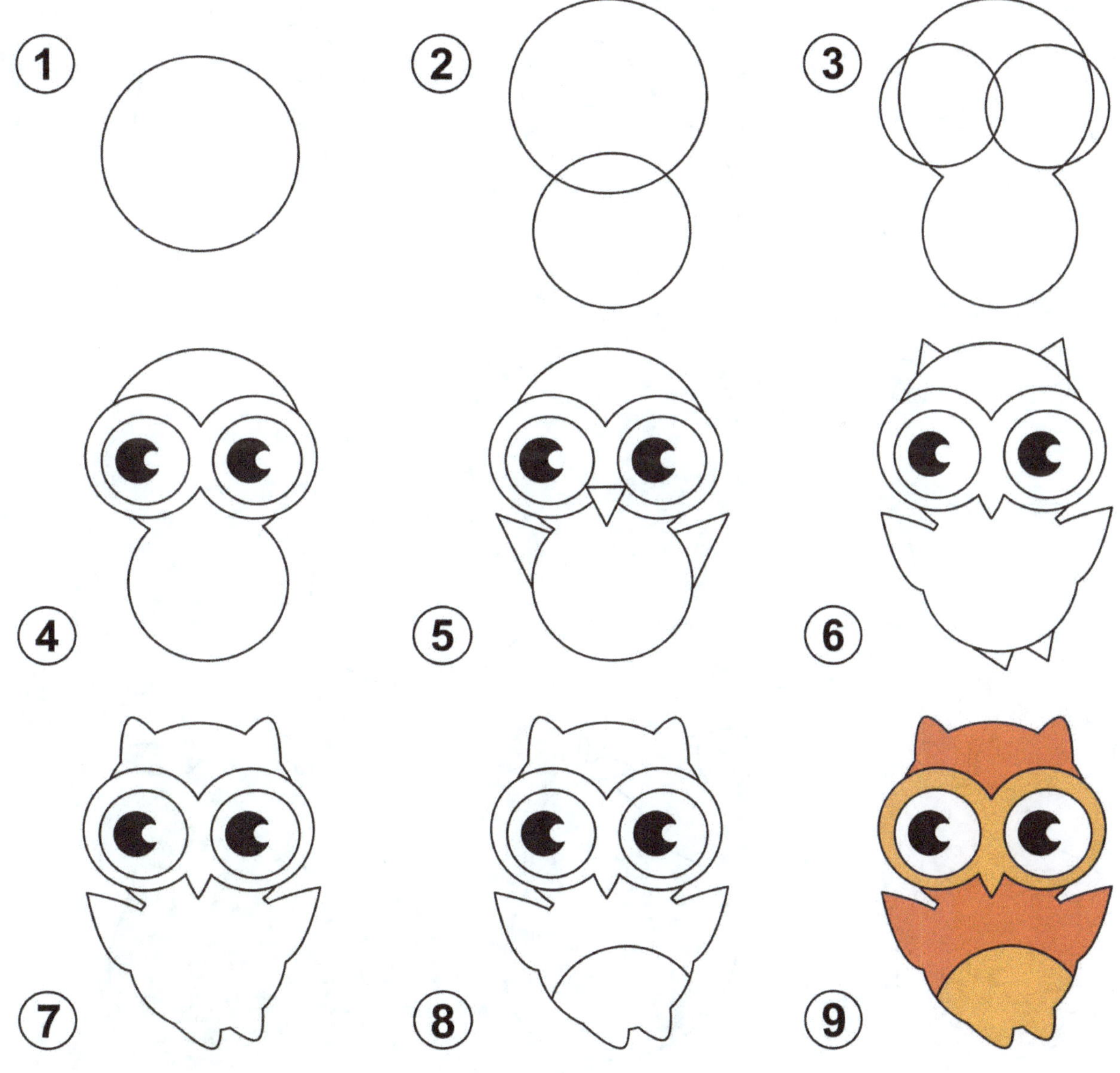

Pear

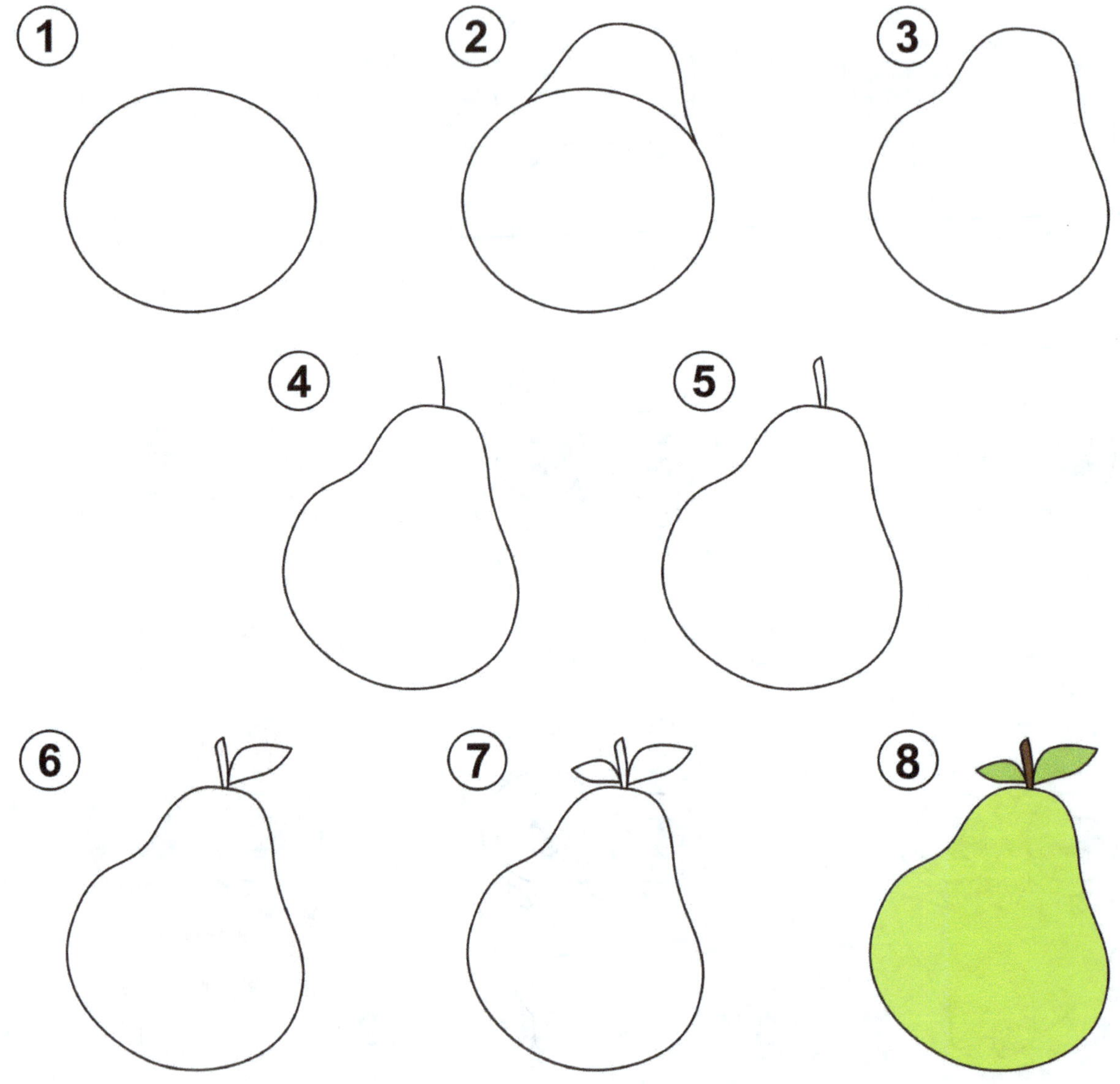

Pink bird

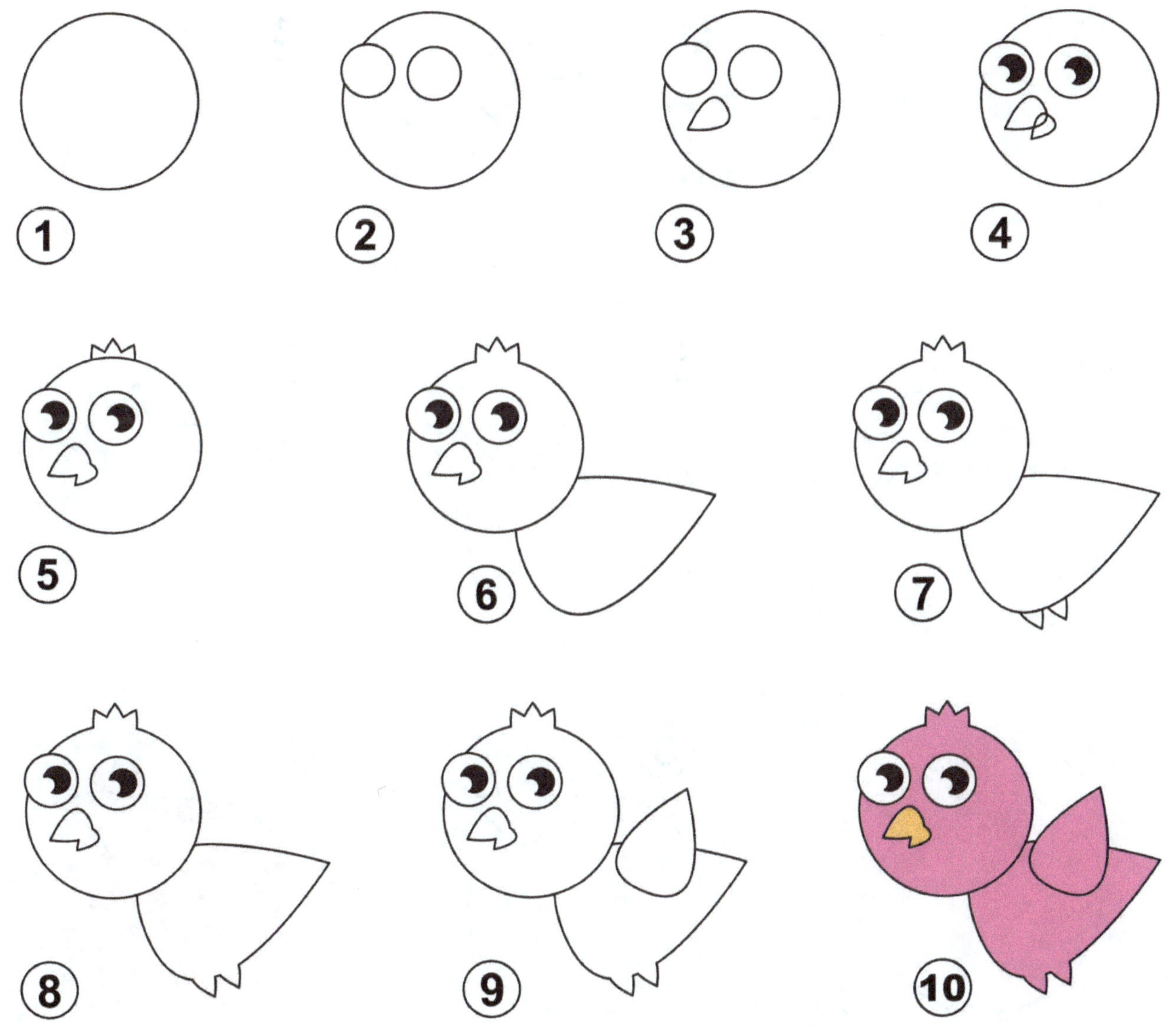

Pomegranate

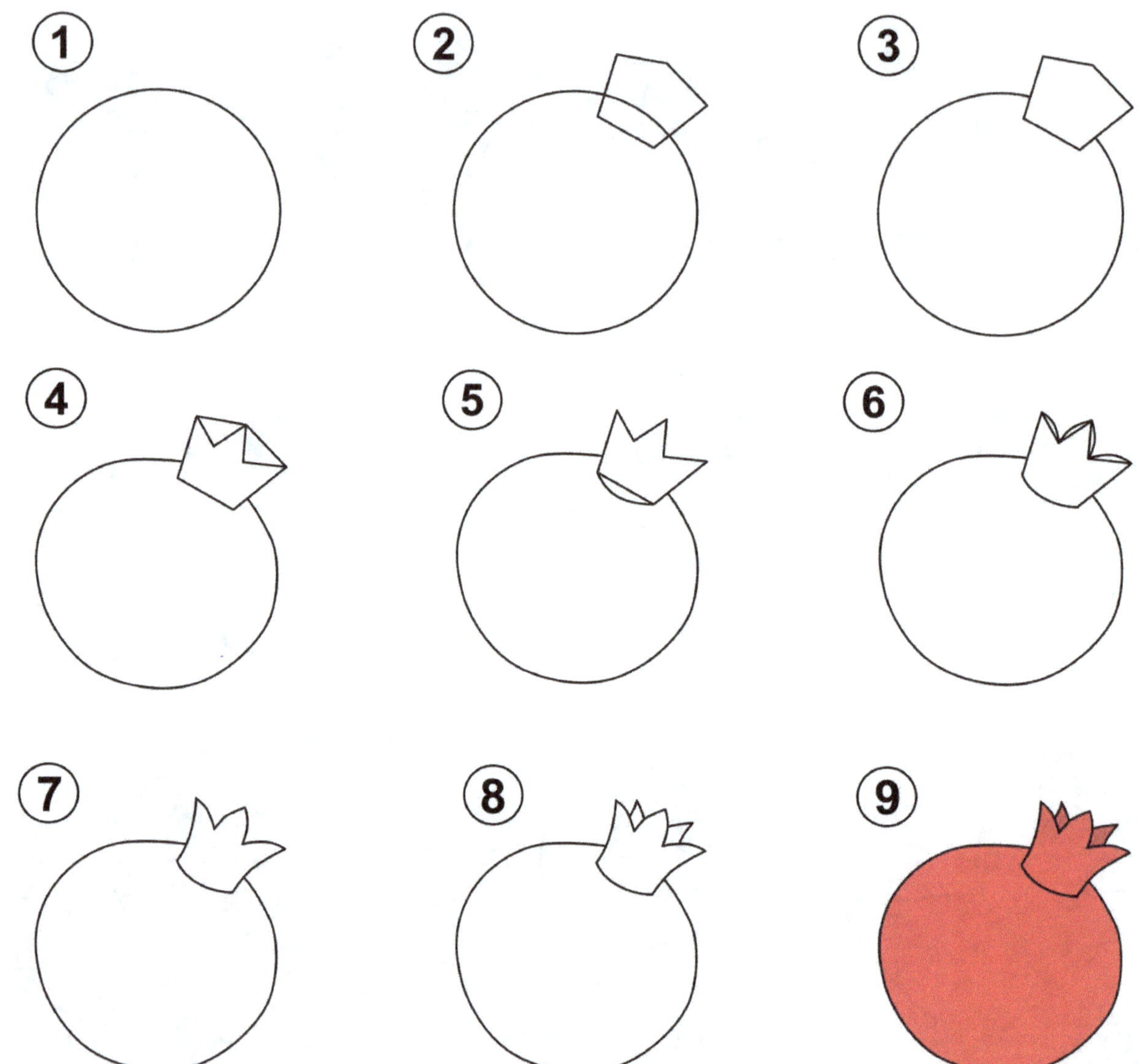

Pot flower

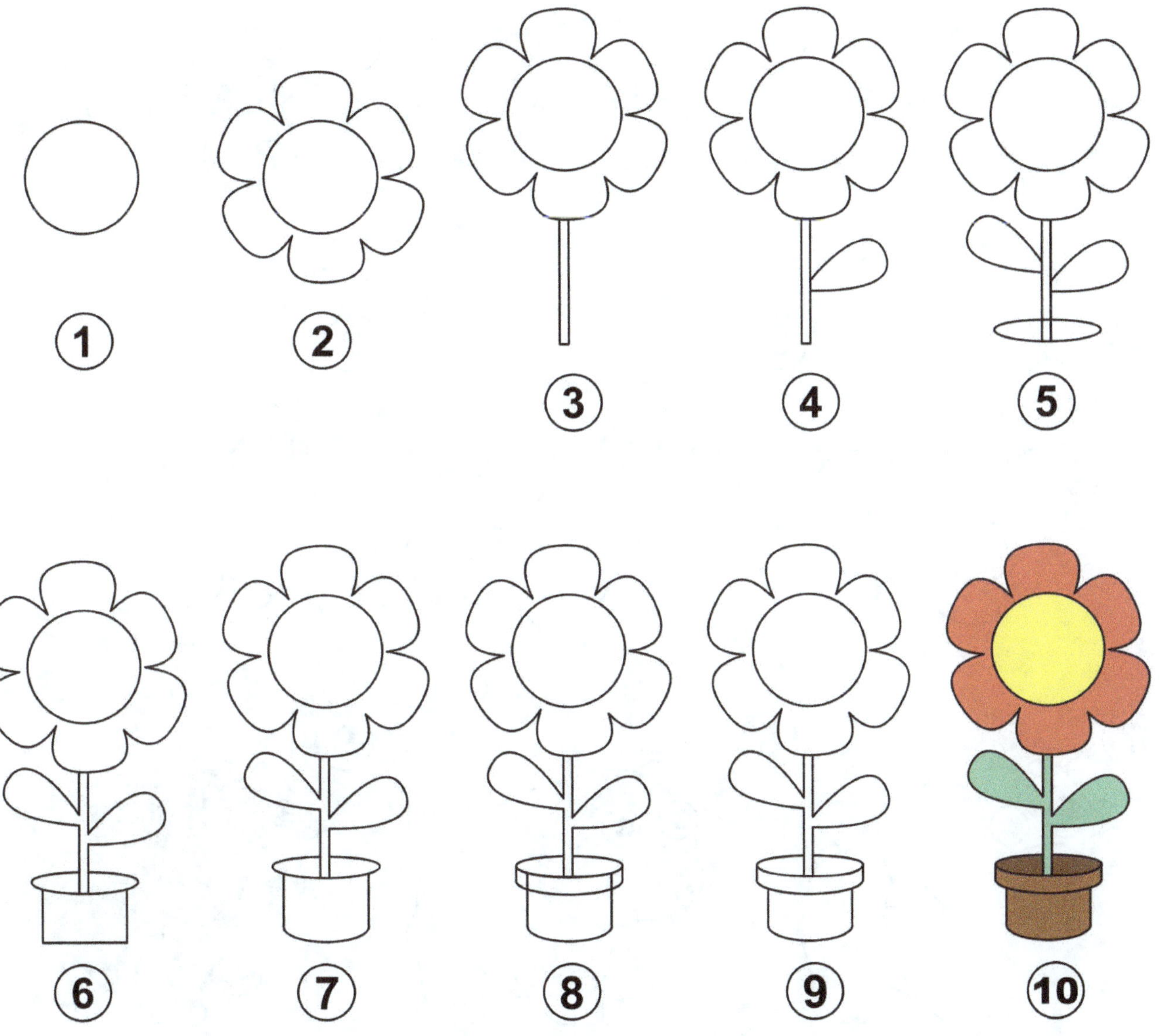

Puppy

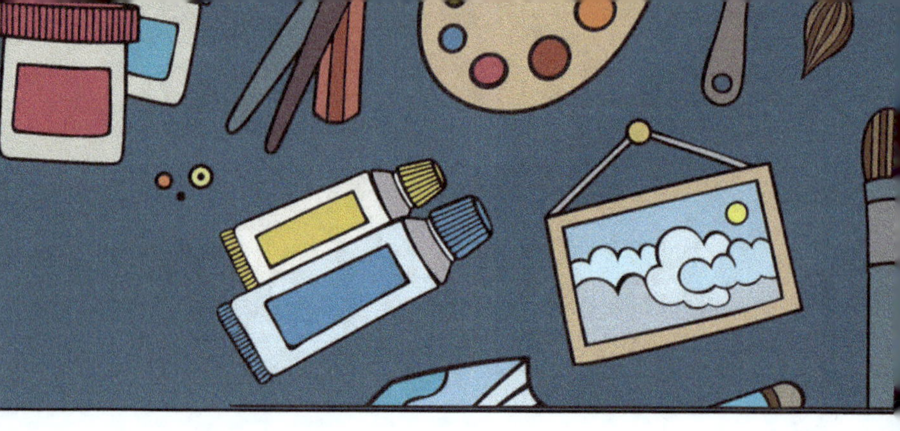

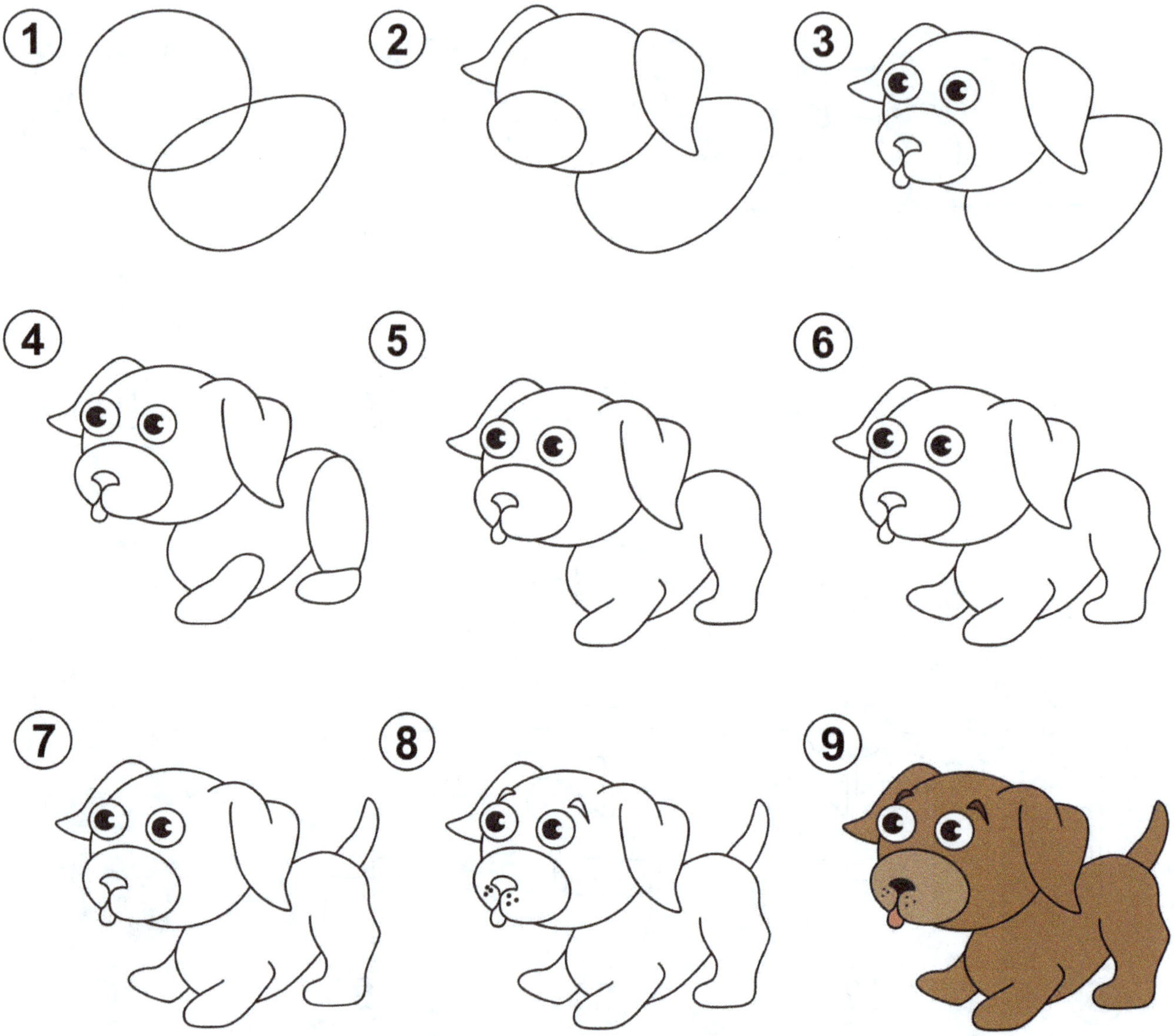

Rabbit

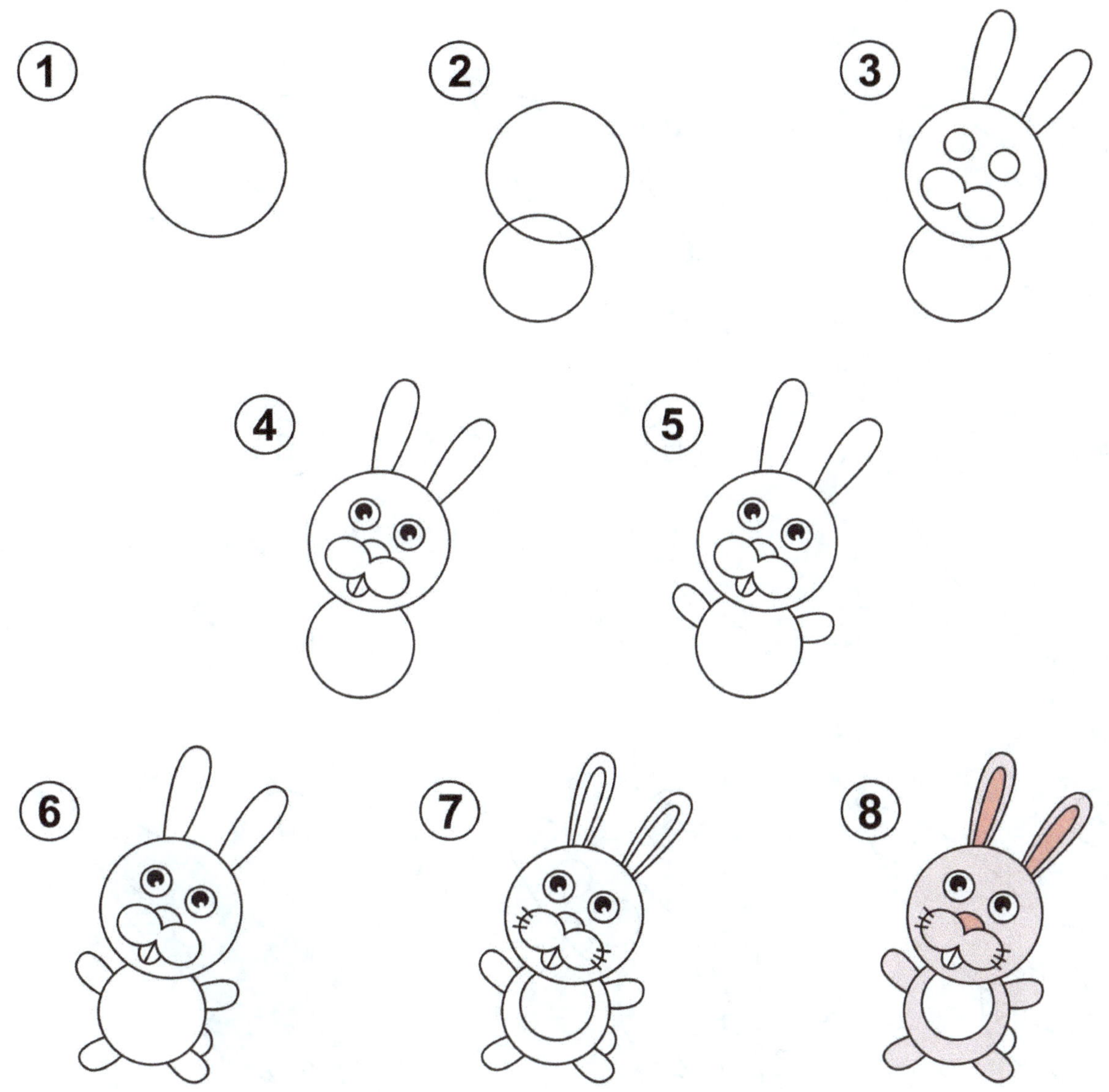

Rocket

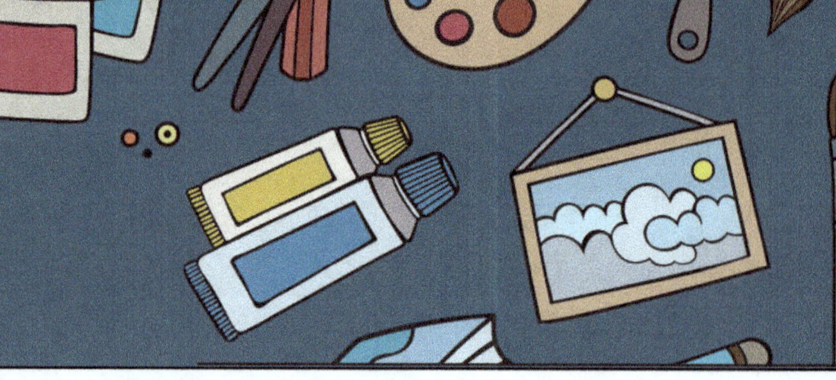

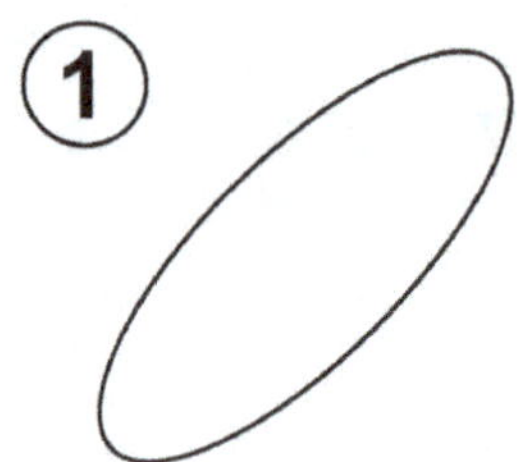

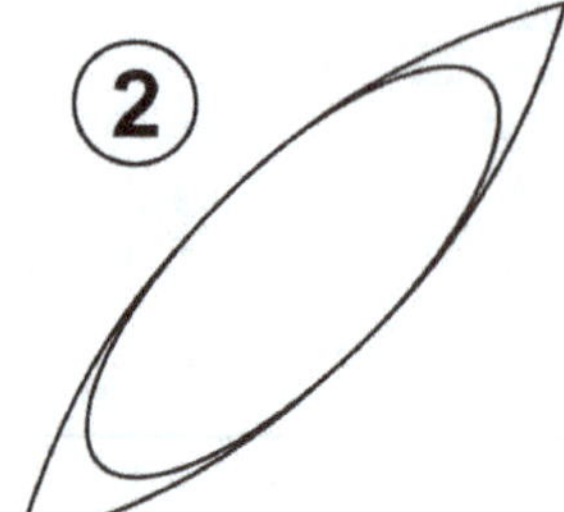

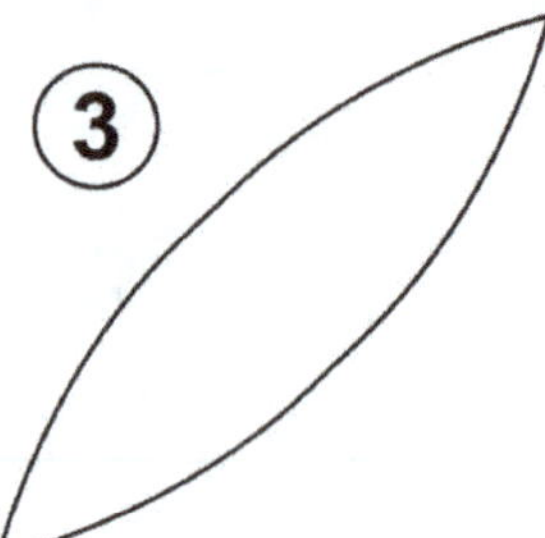

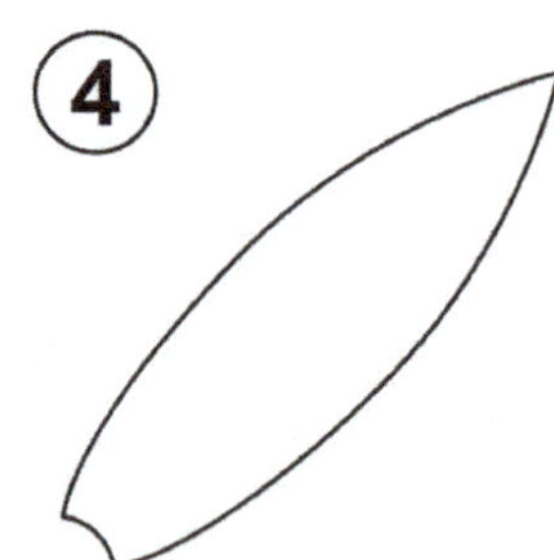

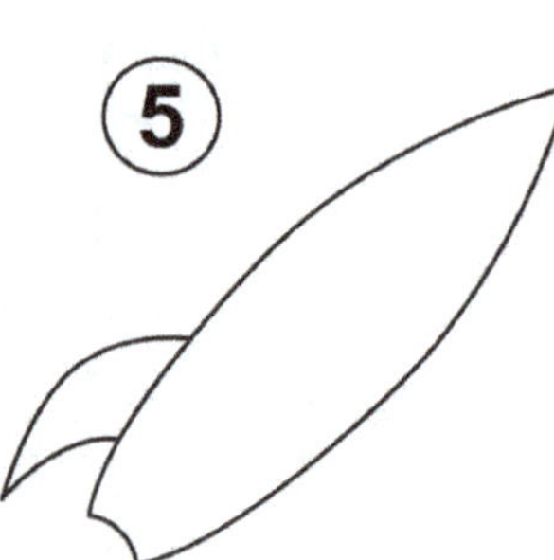

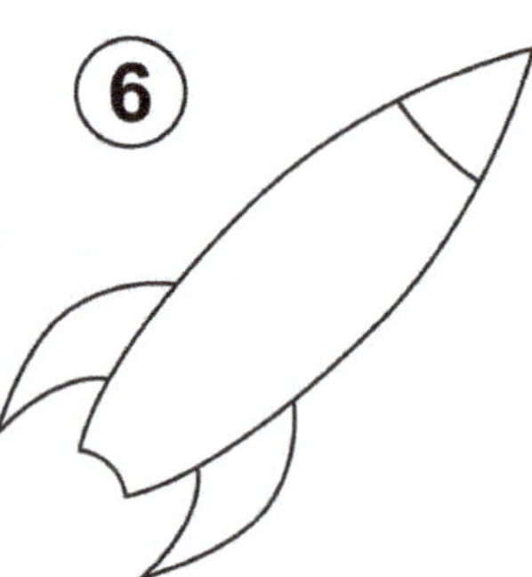

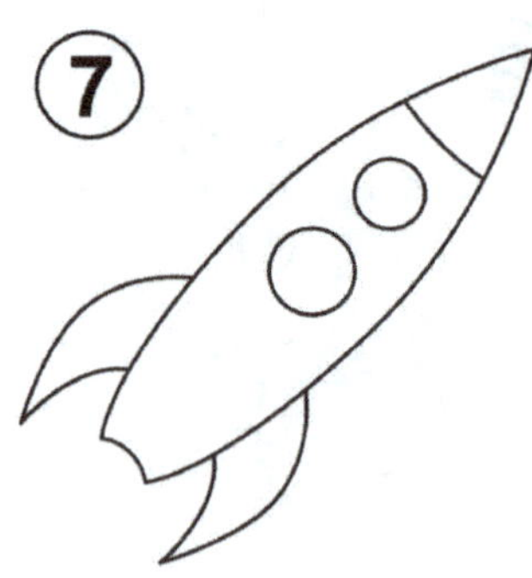

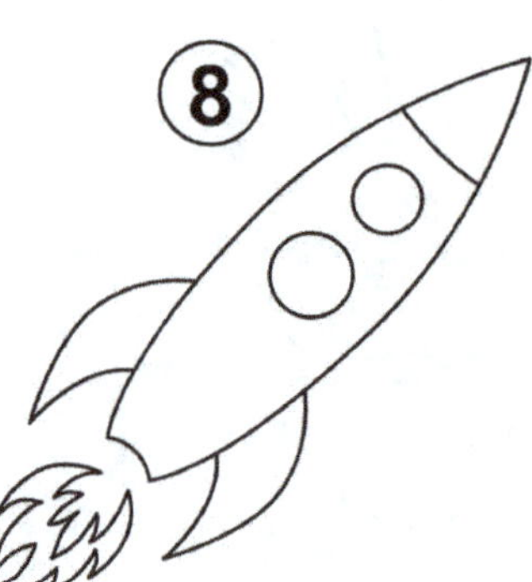

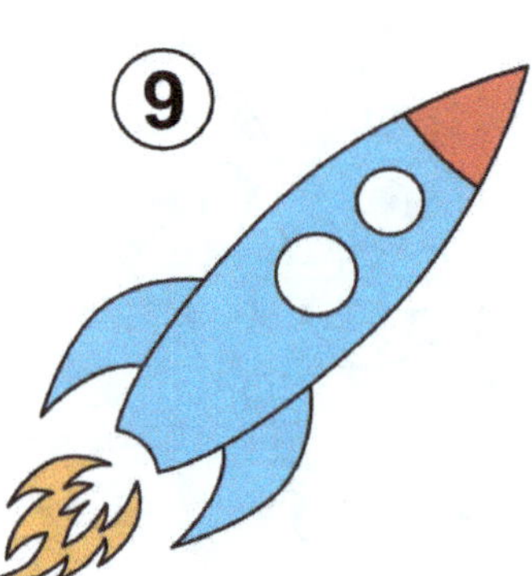

Snake

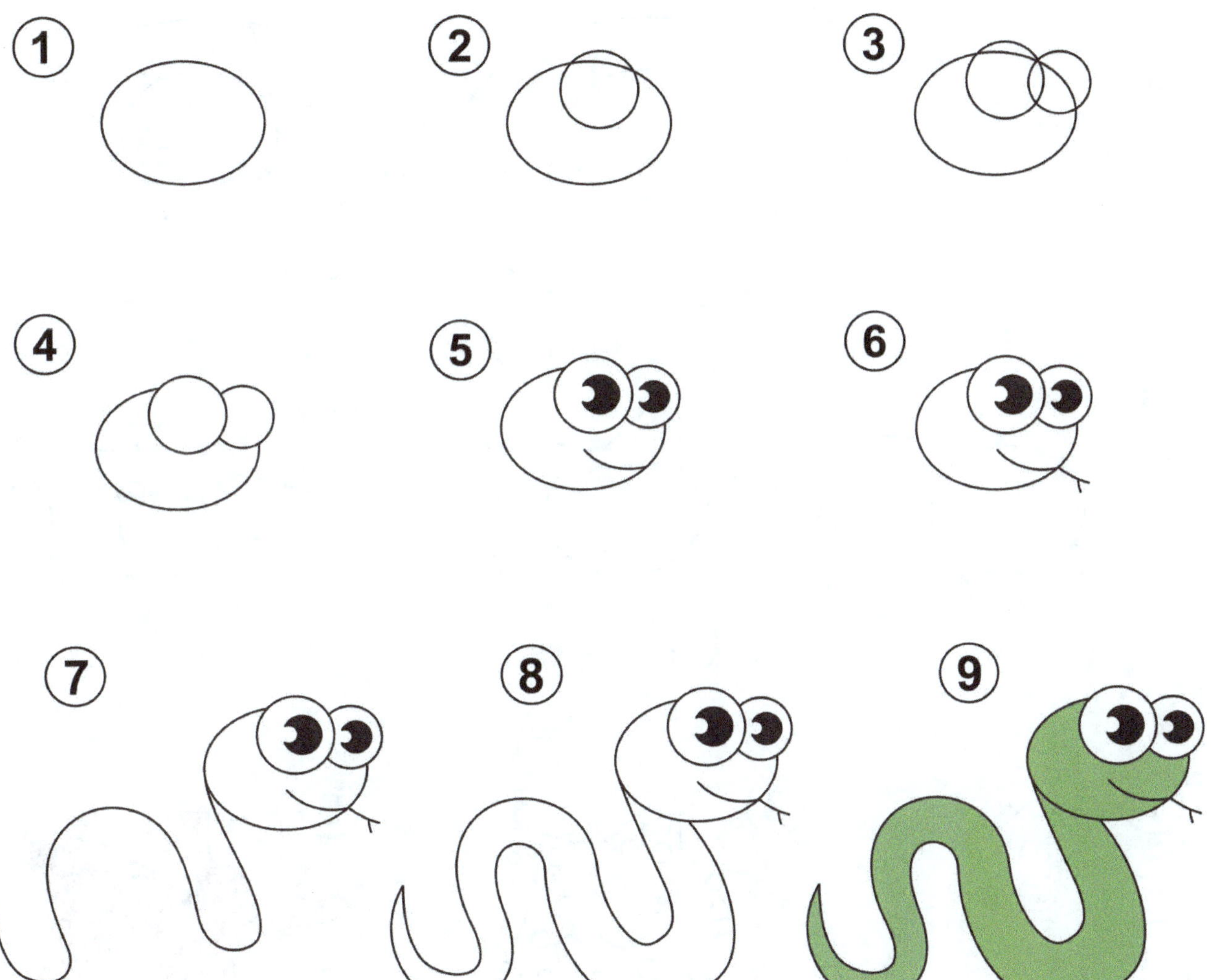

Starfish

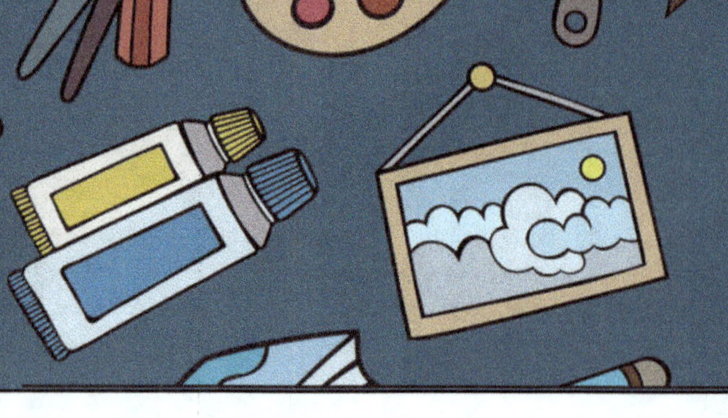

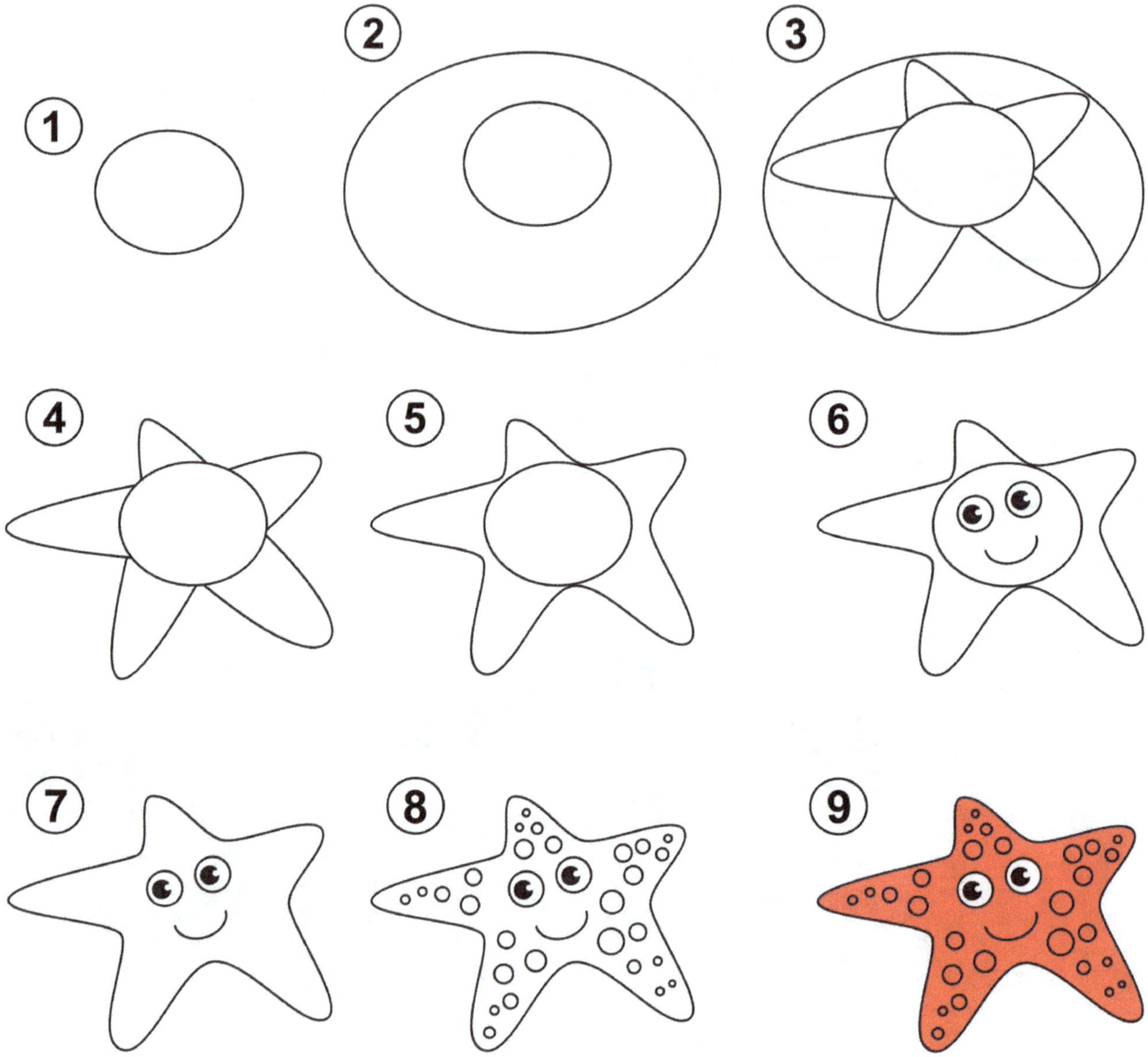

Sun

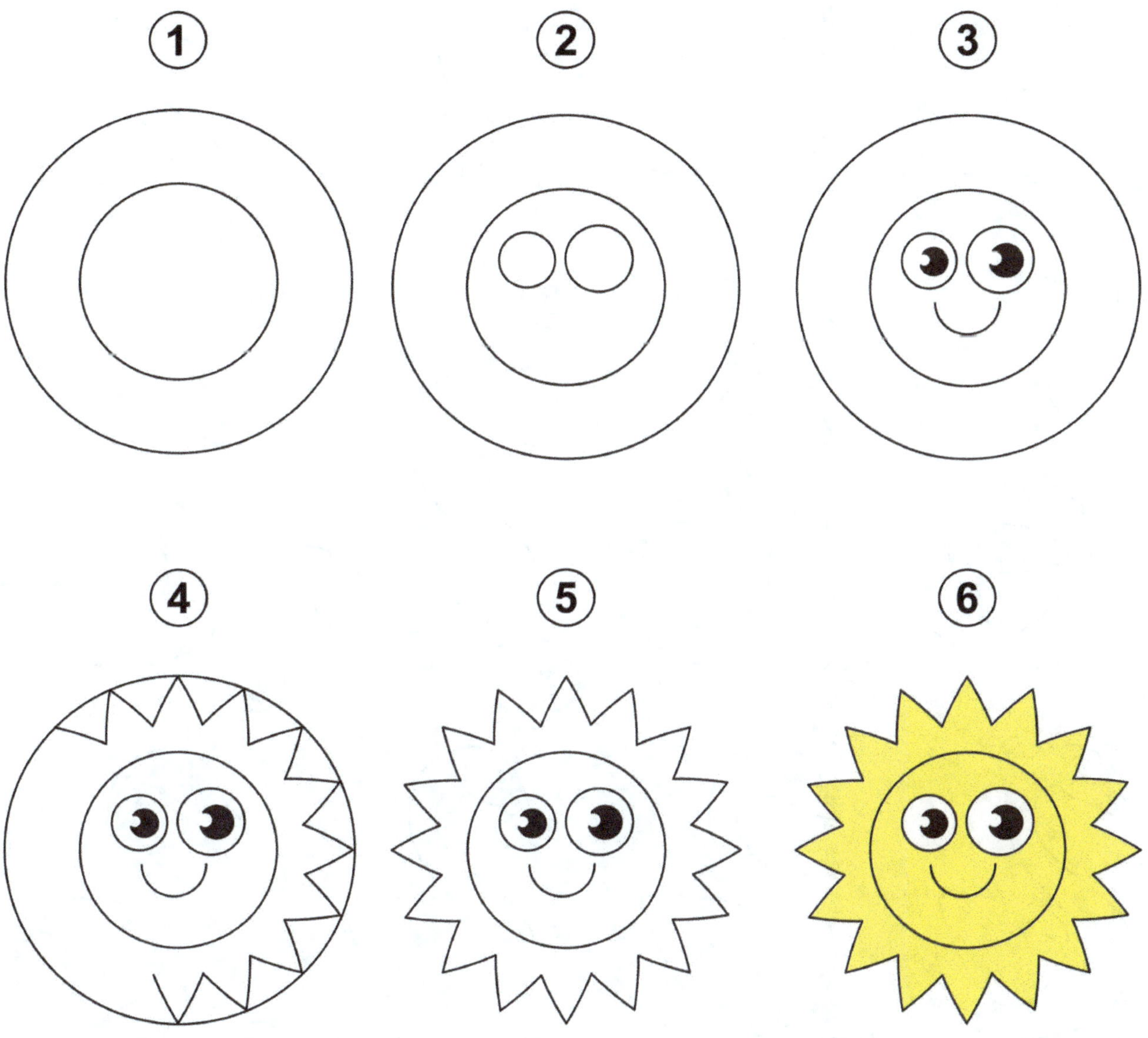

Swan

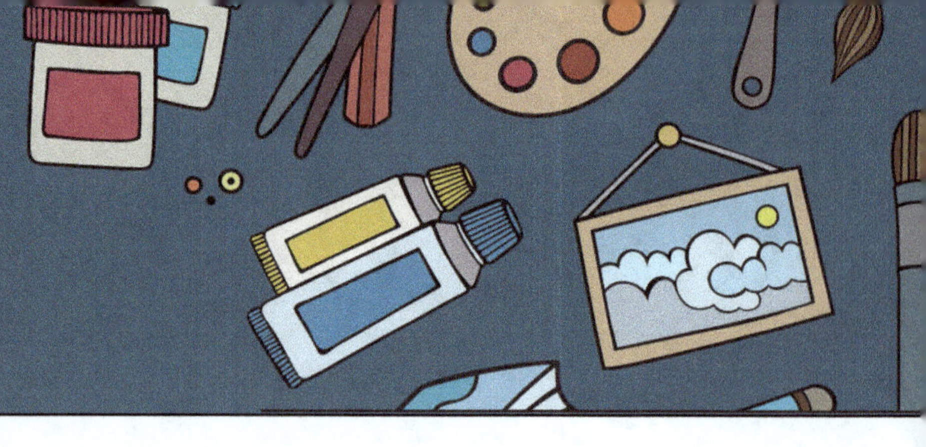

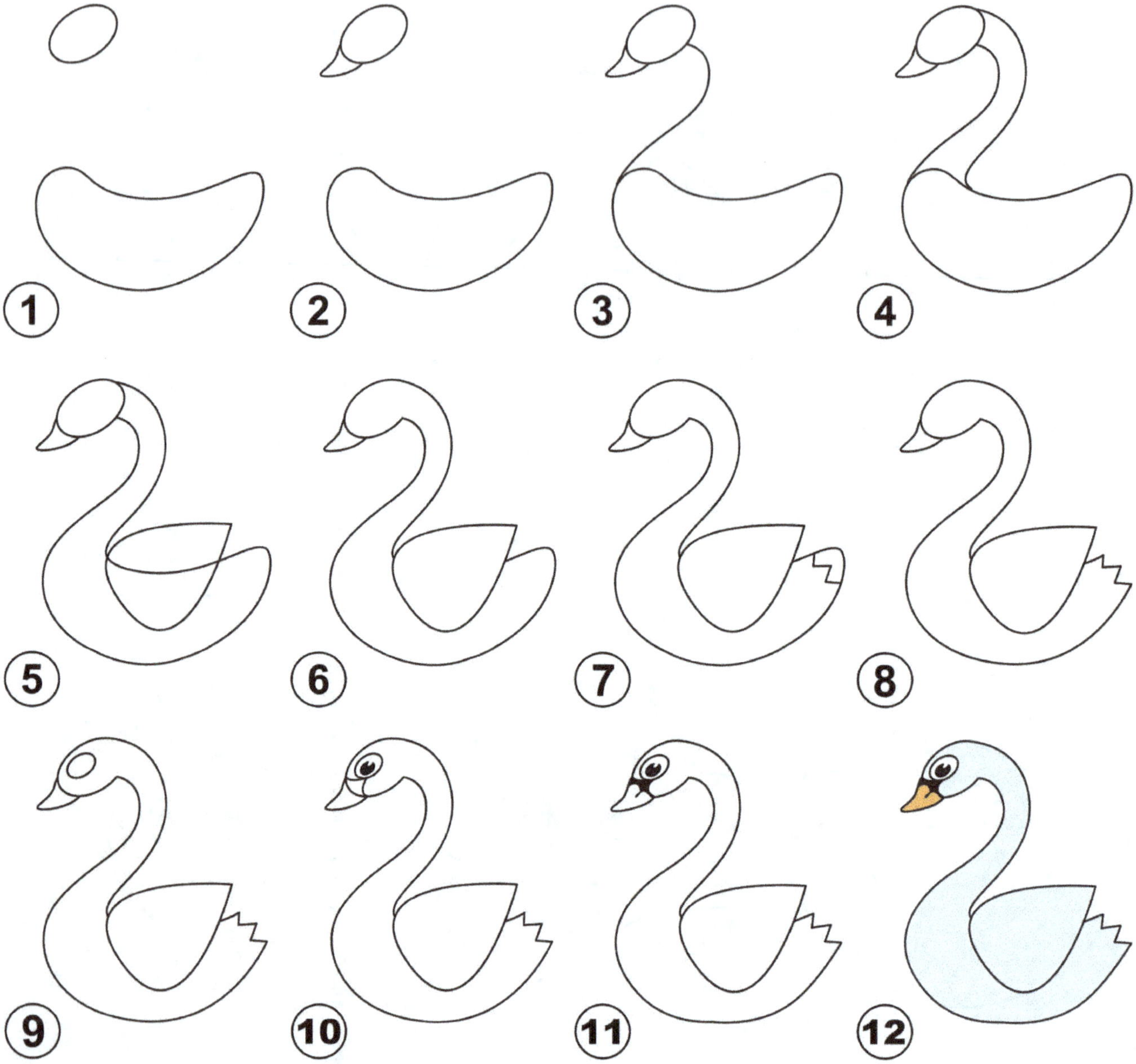

1

2

3

4

5

6

7

8

9

10

11

12

Toad stool

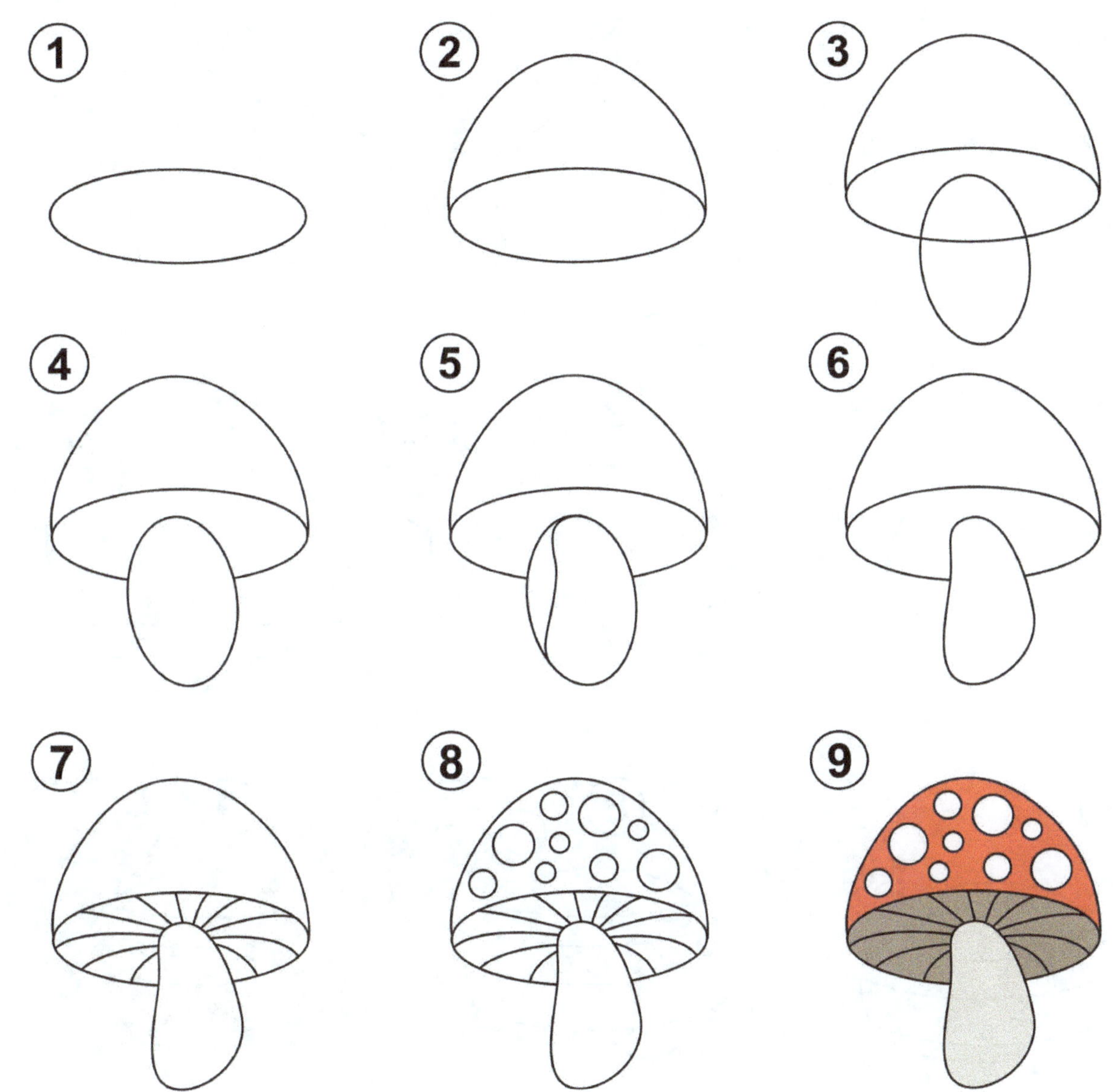

Turtle

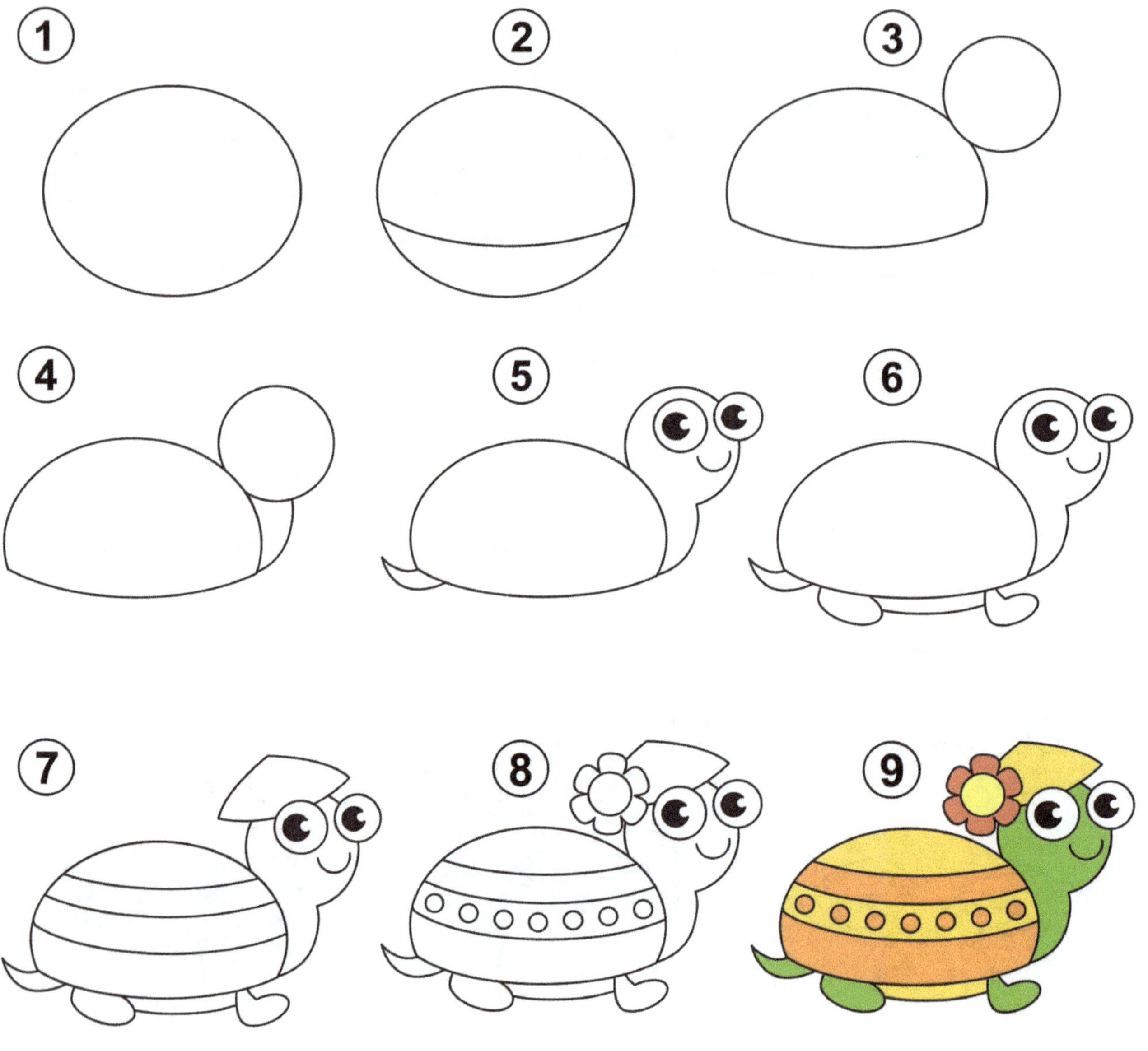

Umbrella

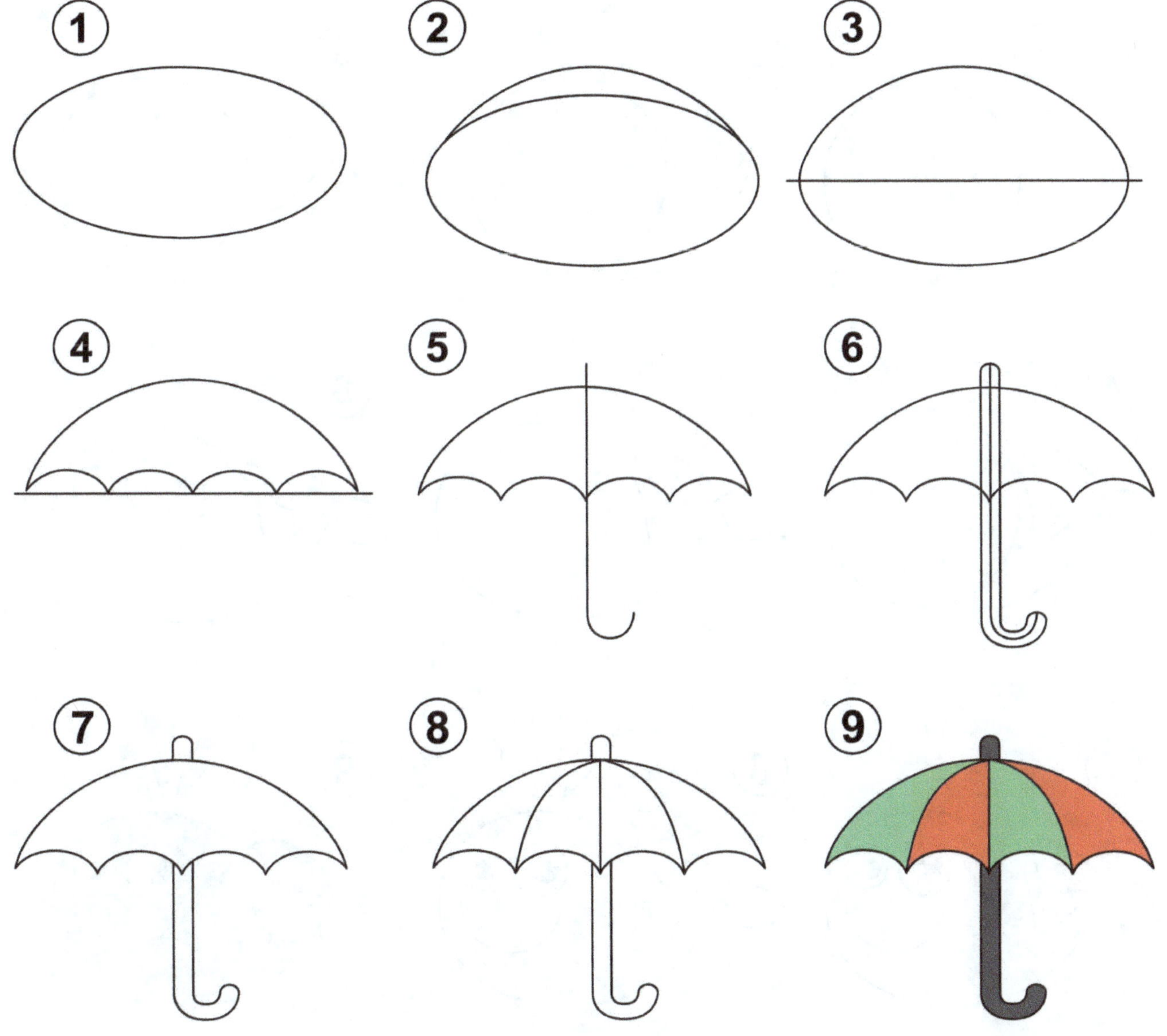

Whale

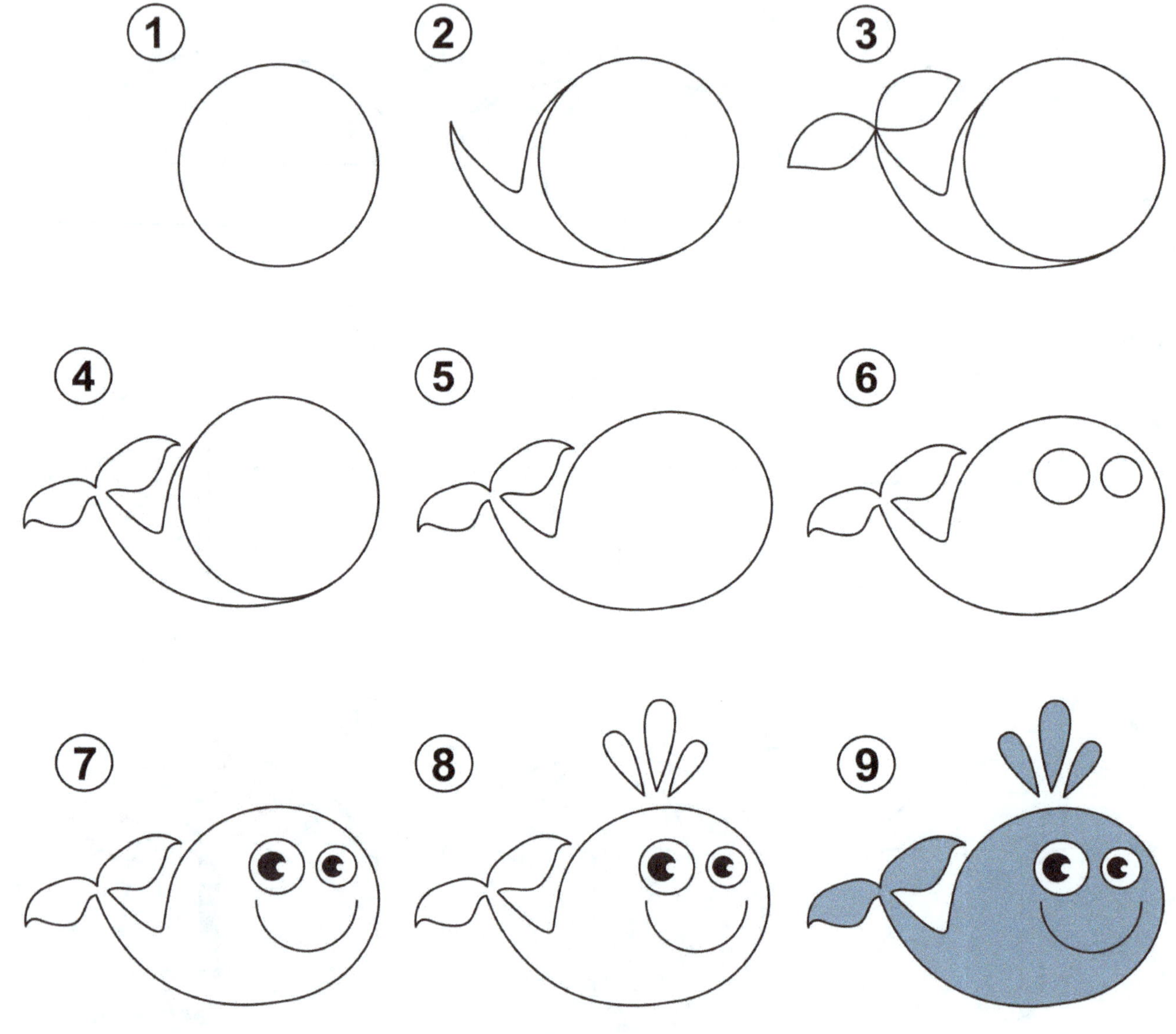

Yak

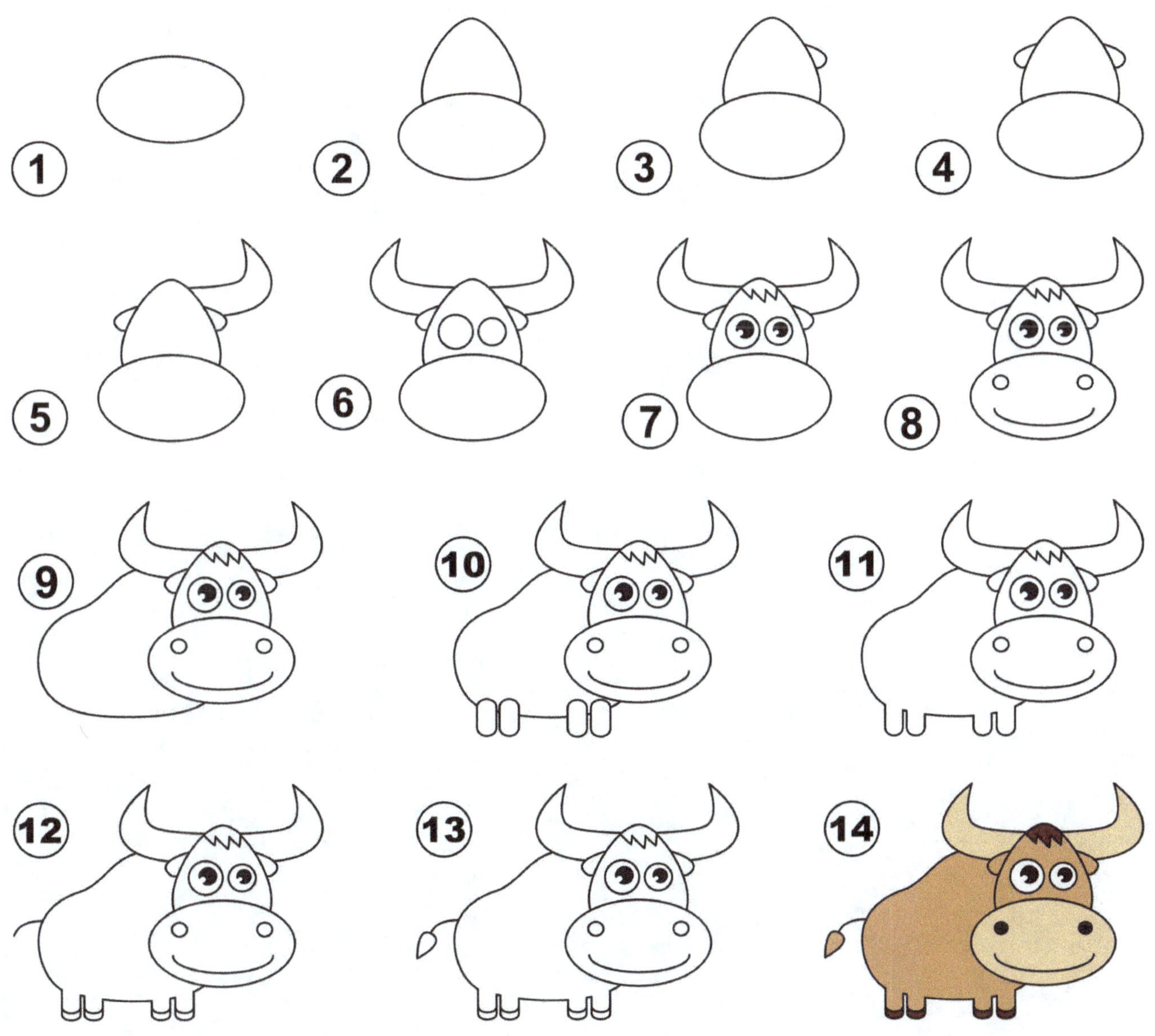